Buy t
France

*How to invest in French property
for pleasure and profit*

CLIVE KRISTEN

howtobooks

Published in 2002 by
How To Books Ltd, 3 Newtec Place,
Magdalen Road, Oxford, OX4 1RE, United Kingdom.
Tel: (01865) 793806. Fax: (01865) 248780.
email: info@howtobooks.co.uk
www.howtobooks.co.uk

All rights reserved. No part of this work may be reproduced
or stored in an information retrieval system (other than for
purposes of review), without the express permission of the
publisher in writing.

© Copyright 2003 Clive Kristen

First edition 2003
Reprinted 2004
Reprinted with amendments 2005

British Library Cataloguing in Publication Data
A catalogue record for this book is available from
the British Library.

Produced for How To Books by Deer Park Productions, Tavistock
Typeset by Anneset, Weston-super-Mare, North Somerset
Cover design by Baseline Arts Ltd., Oxford
Printed and bound by Cromwell Press, Trowbridge, Wiltshire

NOTE: The material contained in this book is set out in good
faith for general guidance and no liability can be accepted
for loss or expense incurred as a result of relying in particular
circumstances on statements made in the book. The laws and
regulations are complex and liable to change, and readers should
check the current position with the relevant authorities before
making personal arrangements.

Contents

Contents

Figures and Tables

Introduction

Interest in French residential property has never been greater. Prices are lower than in the UK, and the French culture and climate are powerful incentives to both renters and buyers. There is now a heightened interest in the French 'buy to let' market. This is in part because it has become increasingly difficult to operate this kind of business profitably in the UK. In December 2002, Richard Donnell, the head of UK residential research at FDP Savills, told *The Sunday Times* that average net yields were 2.8% in central London, 4% in Greater London and between 4.5% and 5% in the South-East. Whilst, at the same time, the picture was rosier in some other corners of the UK, the point was nevertheless made. And, though there are still good reasons for buying UK property as investment, 'buy to let' is no longer high on the list.

Three years on this remains substantively the same. Even the fact that London rentals grew by almost 5% in 2004 is seen by pundits as a blip – brought about by falling property values and an increase in demand created by those 'in between' or 'undecided' about their next foray into the property market. The bull point is this – the UK buy to let market remains uncertain in terms of making a reasonable return on the investment.

This was the genesis of this book. In purely practical terms it began, in part, as a reworking of short sections from the latest edition of a sister volume – *Buying a Property in France*. This was necessary because some core information was equally applicable. Where this has occurred, the detail has been tailored and updated with 'buy to let' in mind. And, having begun with the broad canvas, substantive sections of this volume were then generated by focused research on the 'buy to let' market. I believe the reader will find the sections on the French regions, the letting options, financing and setting up the business, the legal and tax implications, and marketing and planning for profit, particularly useful.

The most valuable lesson I have learned along the way is not to believe in business gurus. There are no magic wands or secret formulas. There is no mantra that can guarantee success. All those I know who have succeeded in the French 'buy to let' sector have made their decisions in a careful and informed way.

I have tried in these pages to offer straightforward, practical and independent advice on a broad range of related subjects, based on my experience. This includes the choices that are available when buying, and how to rent, the costs and intricacies of the legal processes, and how to avoid the pitfalls. The intention throughout is to guide the reader into making informed decisions based on personal financial circumstances and expectations. There are choices to be made, some of which should be carefully considered before entering the French property market. But there is nothing to fear – the leap across the Channel is a small one and the market is carefully regulated.

I would like to thank Linzi Bland for working so diligently on the typescript; my wife, Maureen, for again helping me to maintain the flow of revisions; and Owen Jackson for advice on a wide range of financial matters.

Clive Kristen

1

Why France?

France is the most visited country in Europe: ten million British people crossed the Channel in 2002, along with 70 million other visitors. Around half an hour is all it takes on the swiftest routes to begin experiencing something very special. There are warm summer days and lazy evenings with good food and fine wine; there is the sound of the sea and the magic of the mountains. Indeed, there is something for everyone to enjoy in a country where children are made as welcome as their parents. All this perhaps begins to explain why France is also the first choice for many who are considering the 'buy to let' market.

FIRST THOUGHTS

The British invasion

It is not surprising, therefore, that more and more Britons are becoming property owners on the other side of the Channel. The idea is appealing for a number of reasons. France is our nearest neighbour and most of us already have a smattering of the language. Life there seems to go at an easier pace and the climate is generally better than our own. Since 1992, immigration has been easier, and the Channel Tunnel has fulfilled its promise of rapid, if expensive, transport. The *Sea Cat*, the super ferries, and a network of regional airports, make commuting a possibility, whilst modern communications mean that many kinds of businesses can be run effectively from a base on Europe's mainland.

Another attraction is that property values in France are generally below our own. It may be true that there are fewer

1

bargains to be had these days, especially in the more popular regions but, for those who live in the more expensive quarters of the UK, the difference remains quite staggering.

The change in economic conditions since the mid 90s makes buying property to let in France particularly desirable. The slowdown of the world economy has created a deflated stock market. Pension values are collapsing. Low interest rates are a disincentive to investment but an advantage in terms of loans and mortgages. Property values, particularly in the south-east of the UK, remain such that a realistic return on letting is difficult to achieve.

An investment in French property should generate a return on capital of between 5 and 10%. Despite some localised surges in values the French property market is historically stable with prices, despite some recent regional glitches, moving forwards approximately in line with inflation. The buyer therefore has little fear of negative equity.

The present economic climate is in some ways similar to that which helped to generate the first British 'invasion' of France before the Second World War. One downside of this was the formation of British 'enclaves', which accelerated local property price rises and caused resentment. This also means there are now few bargains to be had in areas such as Provence and the Dordogne valley.

Paris has also been historically popular with the British but has never been 'enclaved'. There are still bargains to be had in Paris but the capital is a specialist market which requires specialist advice.

Access by road

In common with most of our European neighbours, France has seen great improvements in road access during the last ten years. Motorways and dual carriageway *routes nationales* join all the major cities and bypass most of the former bottleneck towns. Although some of the more recently developed motorways are toll roads, it is generally well worth paying for rapid transport between major centres. The motorways have frequent and comfortable *aires* for stretching your legs, relaxation, and even taking a shower. Some of these *aires* have refuelling facilities and modest but inexpensive restaurants, in keeping with the demands of tourism.

Table 1.1 Mileage chart

	Calais	Cherbourg	Le Havre	St. Malo	Roscoff
Amiens	55	180	110	235	330
Caen	220	85	70	115	210
Rennes	290	150	135	50	280
Tours	325	215	190	180	275
Saintes	465	345	330	180	450
Souillac	500	430	420	370	440
Mont de					
Marsan	625	480	490	400	470
Avignon	650	570	570	590	680
Dijon	490	500	410	470	460
Colmar	400	540	430	540	640

Access by Air

France has more airports of international standard than any other European country. However, London apart, access from Britain's regions is patchy and some low-cost operators use airports which are miles away from the cities they purport to serve.

Many provincial British airports have flights direct to their French regional counterparts. Although air transport to France has been historically expensive, the situation has changed because of the low-cost alternatives. If Geneva, for these purposes, is included as a 'French regional airport' there were 24 principal low-cost destinations as of November 2004. Table 1.2 is a 'snapshot' of these.

3

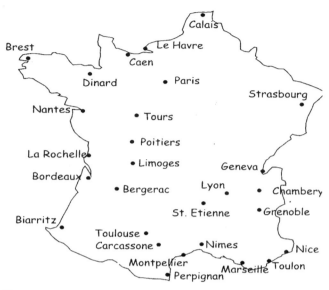

Figure 1.1 Map of principal low-cost destinations.

A number of generally smaller, local airports, all with connections to the UK have been added to the aviation map recently. These, which are themselves a 'snapshot' of the recent surge of British property buying in France, include :

Agen	Dijon	Pau
Angouleme	Dunkerque	Perigeux
Annency	Epinal	Perpignan
Aurillac	Gap	Quimper
Avignon	Lannion	Roanne
Beziers	Le Puy	Rodez
Brive	Le Touquet	Roscoff
Chambery	Lille	Rouen
Cherbourg	Lorient	St Tropez
Clermont Ferrand	Lourdes	St. Brieuc
Deauville	Metx/Nancy	Vichy
Dieppe	Montlucon	

4

Figure 1.2 Airports

Figure 1.2 shows the principal airports, with direct flights to France, in England, Scotland and Wales. One of the best websites for up to date information on routes and prices is www.lastminute.com

Access by rail

The French national railway system – the SNCF – offers a frequent and efficient train service, even to small towns and villages. The new inter-city fast train network – the TGV – is one of the most remarkable and successful engineering projects of modern times. It cost billions. The French are extremely proud of it.

For those familiar with the cost and vagaries of rail travel in the UK the French railway experience is a delight even in anticipation. On a mile-for-mile basis, rail transport in France is around half the cost of the UK.

Climate

Climate is a factor overlooked at your peril if you intend to purchase property in France. It affects not only your own enjoyment of the property but its letting potential. France, as the largest country in Western Europe, also has considerable regional variations in climate.

We tend to think of France as being warmer and sunnier than Britain as it lies to the south. But this is not all together true: Calais, for instance, is more northerly, and considerably colder and wetter than Plymouth.

Much of France lies in the northern temperate zone and is affected by the prevailing westerlies of the Atlantic. The Gulf Stream plays a significant part in determining the coastal climate. Brest, in the north of Brittany, enjoys similar winter temperatures to the Mediterranean resorts but is very much wetter, and subject to fierce Atlantic gales. The climate of the north and western regions of France is similar to that of Devon and Cornwall.

South of a line which roughly parallels the River Loire, the influence of the Mediterranean increases, and the climate is generally warmer and drier. The east of the country towards the Alps has a more typically European climate, with a greater variation in seasonal temperatures. Both the Alps and the Pyrenees have climates which can be severe in the winter and uncertain even in the summer months. The Jura, it is alleged, has two seasons: summer – which lasts about six weeks – and winter. The central zone of France has the greatest temperature

Table 1.2 Average maximum and minimum temperatures

| | January | | August | |
	Maximum	Minimum	Maximum	Minimum
Biarritz	12	6	24	16
Nantes	7	2	25	13
Nice	14	6	30	20
Paris	7	1	22	11

variation: Limoges, for instance, can vary by up to 50°C during the course of the year (typically up to 35°C in August and down to –15°C January/February). One compensation for these severe winters is that they are generally short. It should be pointed out that, regardless of climatic variation, the Alps and to a lesser extent, the Jura, is a special case in terms of potential letting values. Because of skiing in the winter and general tourism in the summer, a ten-month season (normally excluding October and November) is possible, and roads are kept open in a way which would seem almost unbelievable in the UK. The French are neither shocked nor surprised by accumulations of snow in hilly areas in the winter months.

TO BUY OR NOT TO BUY

Buy in haste; repent at leisure

Buying to let should be approached with some caution. This is particularly true if the purchaser intends to enjoy the property, for part of the year, himself.

Prospective purchasers are therefore strongly advised to first experience the letting process for themselves. Whereas it may be considered prudent not to buy a motor vehicle without having first enjoyed a test drive, it is surprising how many do not approach buying to let in the same way. In France they call it 'leaving your brains behind on the plane'.

Rent first

Short-term renting, especially at peak holiday and season periods, can be pricey, but is worthwhile. Longer arrangements – over a period of six months or more – are worth considering too.

French estate agents act for the property owners. The lessee (the person renting the property) will be offered a contract with conditions that have become more or less standardised since the act of December 1986. Renting has other advantages:

- You are not tying up capital or borrowing large sums of money.
- You have a chance to research the local property market.
- You have time to find out how well you and your family adapt to a new way of life.
- You can see whether letting in winter is a real possibility in the area you are considering.
- You can begin drawing up a marketing portfolio for the area you have chosen.

Home Swapping

Home swapping has become a popular alternative to renting.
The established internet market leader is **www.homelink.org.uk** They charge a one-off fee of around €150. Their site has literally thousands of listings and they translate your entry into a number of European languages. The more recently established **www.homeswap.com** and **www.trading-homes.uk** each charge around €75. There are also some well-designed free sites such as **www.peopletraveltheworld.com** and **www.sabbaticalhomes.com**

It is worth noting that home swappers are every bit as honest as those who place personal profiles in lonely hearts' columns. A three-bedroomed terraced house in Walsall, therefore becomes, '*a comfortable three-bedroomed family home close to an international airport with easy access to Shakespeare's Stratford, the sunny pastures of Shropshire, and the lush green valleys of Wales*'.

A Second Home

If your 'buy to let' is also to be your second home, ask yourself the following questions:

- Will you get adequate use of the property? Remember that a second home is an all-year-round expense.

- Will you really want to spend all your holidays in the same place?
- Will the travelling put you off taking short breaks there? And, in winter, are you prepared to accept that a short break may be just long enough to properly warm through and air the property?
- What size property do you really require? Do you honestly need five extra bedrooms for all those friends and family who say they may visit?
- How much of your holiday time are you prepared to devote to repairs, decorating, cleaning gutters and other routine maintenance tasks?
- How will you prioritise the use of the property among your family, friends and paying guests?
- If the property is primarily for letting, how will this affect your mortgage and tax position?
- Will you require the services of a caretaker, gardener or cleaner?
- Who will oversee repairs and renovations in your absence?
- What special arrangements need to made for security when the property is unoccupied? Britain does not have the monopoly on crime, and empty property is attractive to criminals, particularly in rural areas. Worse still, many household insurance policies are invalid if a property is unoccupied for more than 30 days, and power cuts and freezing pipes are more common in France than in the UK.

Need to know

Before you begin looking for property in France there are a number of things you need to know about. These include:

- personal taxation
- registration tax
- Capital Gains tax
- rights as a European citizen

- working in France
- estate agents and *notaires*
- building in France
- banking and finance
- disputes and litigation
- maintaining the vernacular
- the legal process of purchase and letting
- surveys and planning permission
- the renting and running of your property in your absence
- your legal responsibilities
- the economics and logistics of running a successful letting business.

Later sections of this book deal with each of these.

Do not be put off by what may seem to be an encyclopaedia of knowledge. The French do things differently, but their approach is generally based on common sense, and the legal process is designed to protect you.

2

Where and What to Buy

Before diving into the French property market there are a number of things to consider.

THE FRENCH PROPERTY MARKET

Property Values

There is no real evidence to suggest that the French employ a dual pricing policy. The French are, however surprised (and frequently highly delighted) at the amount that the British are prepared to pay. Advertised prices, particularly in areas popular with the British, can reflect this.

A potential French buyer regards an advertised price, particularly on an older property, as a starting point for negotiation. He knows that the asking price is optimistic. He also knows that, although prices are higher in the south, this creates more room for manoeuvre. There is nothing to prevent a potential UK buyer from taking a similarly robust approach. Here are some general pointers:

- New properties are more expensive than older ones but they enjoy tax breaks and benefits.
- Although the asking price is invariably more than the selling price it may be difficult to judge how much room there is to negotiate.
- Be prepared to walk away from a deal whilst showing enthusiasm for the property itself. Leave a telephone number and wait for a call.
- Never express interest in the land that the property is built

on. The French are used to large plots and do not see this as significant.

- The French estate agent (*agent immobilier*) is aware of the buying whims of their UK customers. In some areas you will find agents with window displays in English. This is not because of the *entente cordiale*.
- New apartments and condominiums are expensive. They are invariably built on prime sites in fashionable areas.
- Older apartments and condominiums are variably priced. Much depends on the age and condition of the building as a whole.
- Property values decrease according to remoteness. In the same region you may find a large country house in the same price bracket as a seaside apartment.
- Certain regions, particularly towns and villages, and even certain streets, are 'fashionable'. This factor should be built into the cost equation.
- Sometimes, the seller pays the estate agent's costs. Do not be deceived. The asking price has been rounded up to take account of this.
- You can avoid agent's charges by buying direct. Local newspapers and cards placed in newsagents and supermarkets are a good place to start.
- A small garden has a different meaning on the other side of the channel. We tend to think of something larger than a window box; they regard it as something which does not require the services of a full-time gardener.
- Registration fees are lower on properties that are less than five years old.
- The legal process of purchase, including surveys and planning applications, will add between 10 and 15 per cent to the purchase price.

What choice is there?

There is property in France to suit all pockets and lifestyles; but some of these properties are less suitable than others in the buying to rent market.

The most common type of French property – the *pavillon* – is primarily designed for a large live-in family. The *pavillon* often features a substantial '*sous sol*' which will swallow three cars and any number of household appliances, and will still have copious storage areas for everything from winter logs to bags of road salt, garden implements and toys.

In the 'buy to let' market, it is tempting to consider something either larger or smaller than the *pavillon*. If larger, the property may divide into owner's accommodation and a *gîte* for letting. A smaller property – an apartment perhaps – will make the most economic use of space.

French estate agents maintain databases of property that are more up to date than the free property guides racked up outside the offices. Always ask for a list rather than a guide and ask to be added to the mailing and email lists.

Some agents place sample advertisements in English newspapers and on English language websites. This can be little more than a ruse to add a potential UK buyer to the mailing list. French immobiliers (estate agents) also share national websites. These include **www.pap.fr.com** and **www.entreparticuliers.com**

National surveys of properties linked to these sites are published monthly. The best known of these publications are *Les Annonces Immobilieres* (€2.40 monthly) and *De Particulier à Particulier* (€2.75 bi-monthly). Both these publications are available through French bookshops and newsagents or may be ordered directly via their web sites.

The estate agent's window remains a prime source of information once you have made the decision to buy. Studied carefully, it can tell you almost all you need to know about the local property market. Even if you don't speak French it is possible to work out general facts about a property. French properties are advertised typically as T1 or T3 or T6, etc. This is short for type 1 or type 3 or type 6 – the digit referring to the number of principal rooms. A T4, therefore, could be a three-bedroomed dwelling with a living room or a two-bedroomed one with a separate lounge and dining room.

Here are five properties in and around a pleasant market town on the banks of the Loire. They were featured *'free of agent's charges'* at the same agency in October 2004.

The first is a stone-built property situated approximately 300 metres from the town centre:

> *A traditional house of 130 square metres, 4 bedrooms, fully equipped kitchen, bathroom, 2 WCs. Of very good quality construction with an open fireplace in the lounge and a separate living room. The property has full double glazing, two garages, a cellar and an attic. French windows in the living room give onto 30 square metres of covered terrace and a further 60 square metres of uncovered terrace. The central heating is electric. The property stands in 1620 square metres of land. The garden is walled with mature trees. Asking price €162,000.*

The second is in a small village about ten miles from the same town :

> *A four bedroom split-level property covering 150 square metres. The property features a fully equipped kitchen, two bathrooms and two separate WCs. There is a lounge with a log burning fireplace and separate living room which gives onto a south facing terrace. Heating is by gas. The property, which is constructed on approx. 2000 square metres of land is situated close to local shops in an historic village. Asking price € 127,000*

The third is a modern property constructed close to the town's outer ring-road :

14

Building of recent construction of 90 square metres. There are three bedrooms, a bathroom, separate WC, a family room, heat and sound insulation, a water softener, electric central heating, a small terrace, and a designated parking place covered by CCTV cameras. Asking price €116,000.

Next is a substantial rural property some 12 miles from the town, with the nearest village two miles distant:

Partly renovated farm buildings set in approx. 0.8 hectare with a barn suitable for conversion. The main building consists of five bedrooms, two living rooms, a traditional style kitchen with log-burning stove and back boiler, a vestibule and hallway, one bathroom with WC, separate WC, pantry and cellar. Lean-to garage and log store adjoin main building. Barn approx. 110 square metres' floor space. Small orchard and fishing pond. Gravelled track to main road. Asking price €142,000

And, finally, here is an apartment close to the town centre:

Recently constructed T3 type apartment on third floor of five storey building. Master bedroom with en-suite facilities, separate bathroom and WC. Fitted kitchen with waste disposal. Recessed lighting in living area. Electric central heating. Balcony overlooks historic town square. Underground secure garaging for one vehicle. Additional secure parking by negotiation at extra cost. Asking price €140,000.

Price guidelines

It is impossible to be precise about how much you would expect to pay for a French property. This is because variations within regions themselves can be considerable and, as in the UK, location is everything.

However, in general terms, your money could buy:

Up to €35,000	A barn or a small farmhouse requiring renovation.
Up to €50,000	A studio apartment in a popular resort or a partly restored cottage in a rural area.
Up to €65,000	A substantial farmhouse requiring renovation, a one-bedroomed apartment in a popular town or a partly restored three-bedroomed rural property.
Up to €85,000	A restored three-bedroomed rural property, a modern two-bedroomed property or a three-bedroomed restored farmhouse, a tasteful barn conversion or a one-bedroomed apartment in a popular resort.
Up to €130,000	A fully restored four or five-bedroomed farmhouse, a fully restored rural property with a swimming pool, a two-bedroomed apartment in a popular resort or a tasteful barn conversion with an orchard and pool.
Up to €160,000	A three-bedroomed apartment in a popular resort, a fully restored five-bedroomed farmhouse, a studio apartment in a fashionable part of Paris, a two-bedroomed apartment in the Alps or a small château in need of renovation.
Up to €325,000	A two-bedroomed apartment in the Champs-Elysées, a luxury apartment at a popular resort, a modest but partly restored château, a very respectable villa with a pool in Provence or a luxury three-bedroomed chalet in the Alps.

These prices should be considered in all cases as best value.

A property survey

The following tables may provide more valuable guidelines. They summarise comprehensive returns from ten major towns and their surrounding districts. The prices are an average for various property types and are rounded to the nearest square metre.

It may be helpful to know that a three/four-bedroomed house with a garage is likely to be 180 square metres, a typical three-bedroomed bungalow around 120 square metres, and a holiday style two-bedroomed bungalow around 80 square metres.

Using the tables that follow you could calculate, for example, that the cost of an average-sized (120 square metre) renovated house in the centre of Bordeaux would be: 1380 x 120 = €165,600 and a new property of the same size in the same city centre would be 1770 x 120 = €212,400.

Table 2.1 Town centre house prices

	Unrestored	Renovated	New
Bordeaux	850	1380	1770
Clermont Ferrand	990	1370	1600
Dijon	1095	1265	1625
Lille	870	1325	1755
Lyon	1083	1380	1870
Marseille	640	1150	1640
Nantes	800	1280	1660
Orléans	935	1185	1600
Rouen	880	1380	1800
Strasbourg	1060	1320	1815
Average	**920**	**1303**	**1714**

Table 2.2 Suburban house prices

	Unrestored	Renovated	New
Bordeaux	750	920	1210
Clermont Ferrand	750	950	1220
Dijon	760	900	1240
Lille	730	935	1200
Lyon	800	1060	1390
Marseille	640	915	1170
Nantes	740	980	1220
Orléans	820	1080	1210
Rouen	830	1060	1310
Strasbourg	820	1040	1370
Average	**764**	**984**	**1254**

Table 2.3 Rural house prices

	Unrestored	Renovated	New
Bordeaux	380	610	925
Clermont Ferrand	415	575	875
Dijon	430	540	915
Lille	370	655	925
Lyon	465	645	1075
Marseille	325	530	925
Nantes	390	540	900
Orléans	375	530	730
Rouen	500	510	980
Strasbourg	465	600	960
Average	**411**	**574**	**921**

Price stability

Overall, price stability is predicted to continue, although local demand could again dictate more rapid increases or realignments in values in some areas.

The French property market did not experience the spirals of price inflation that took place in the UK during the 1970s and late 1980's, nor the slump that followed. Prices tend to ease forward gradually in line with building costs, wages and the state of the economy. Over the last 10 years, figures have again shown that the French property prices have risen roughly in line with inflation although some localised increases above these levels have been mistakenly interpreted as indicators of a wider inflationary spiral.

Rental activity

The following lists should provide food for thought. The first is of the departments which have the highest levels of long-term rental activity according to Les Annonces Immobilieres. In each case, the number relates to the department number and the town indicated in brackets is the most popular location. (A map and a full listing of the departments can be found in the appendices.)

Bouches du Rhône 13 (Marseille)	Bas-Rhin 67 (Strasbourg)
Haute Garonne 31 (Toulouse)	Rhône 69 (Lyon)
Isère 38 (Morette)	Paris 75 (Paris)
Meurthe et Moselle 54 (Nancy)	Seine Maritime 76 (Rouen)
Nord 59 (Lille)	Vienne 86 (Poitiers)

The next list is of departments which, again according to Les *Annonces Immobilieres*, appear to have little long-term rental activity:

Ain 1	Landes 40
Alpes-de-Haute-Provence 4	Loir-et-Cher 41
Hautes-Alpes 5	Loire 42
Ardèche 7	Haute Loire 43
Ardennes 8	Lot 46
Ariège 9	Lozère 48
Aube 10	Haute-Marne 52
Aveyron 12	Nièvre 58
Calvados 14	Orne 61
Cantal 15	Pas-de-Calais 62
Corse 20	Haute-Pyrénées 65
Creuse 23	Saône-et-Loire 71

Dordogne 24	Haute-Savoie 74
Drôme 26	Seine-et-Marne 77
Eure-et-Loir 28	Yvelines 78
Gard 30	Tarn-et-Garonne 82
Gers 32	Yonne 89
Indre 36	Territoire de Belfort 90
	Essonne 91

In terms of short-term (holiday) rental, the picture is rather different. Again, according to *Les Annonces Immobilieres,* the most popular locations are listed below. Again, in each case, the number indicates the department, and the town indicated is a particularly popular location.

Alpes-Maritimes 6 (Nice)
Charente Maritime 17 (La Rochelle)
Dordogne 24 (Verteillac)
Gironde 33 (Le Verdonsurmer)
Hérault 34 (Montpellier)
Ille-et-Vilaine 35 (Saint Briac sur Mer)
Isère 38 (Chamrousse)
Jura 39 (Bois d'Amont)
Lot-et-Garonne 47 (Villereale)
Hautes Pyrénées 65 (La Mongie)
Pyrennees-Orientales 66 (Le Barcares)
Savoie 73 (Les Arcs)
Haute-Savoie 74 (Annecy le Vieux)
Var 83 (Frejus)

The following departments appear to have a low level of short-term (holiday) letting activity:

Ain 1	Meurthe-et-Moselle 54
Aisne 2	Meuse 55
Allier 3	Moselle 57
Ariège 9	Nièvre 58

Aube 10	Nord 59
Cher 18	Oise 60
Doubs 25	Pas-de-Calais 62
Eure 27	Bas-Rhin 67
Eure-et-Loire 28	Haut-Rhin 68
Gers 32	Haute-Saône 70
Indre 36	Saône-et-Loire 71
Indre-et-Loire 37	Sarthe 72
Loir-et-Cher 41	Seine-Maritime 76
Loire 42	Seine-et-Marne 77
Loiret 45	Yvelines 78
Lozère 48	Deux-Sèvres 79
Maine-et-Loire 49	Somme 80
Marne 51	Vienne 86
Haute-Marne 52	Haute-Vienne 87
Mayenne 53	Territoire de Belfort 90
	Essonne 91

The above lists should not be regarded as definitive, but as snapshots of rental activity indicated by *Les Annonces Immobilieres* during the spring and summer of 2004. Some general conclusions, however, may be drawn, including the following:

- Certain areas of France have little tradition of either long-term or holiday rental activity.
- In some departments, particularly in the north of France, long-term rental is a relative rarity and holiday rental is equally conspicuous by its absence.
- Certain departments which embrace the Alps, Alpes Maritime, the Vosges and the Pyrenees have a significant share of the holiday rental market, but long-term rental opportunities are thinner on the ground.
- Paris is unusual, in that long-term rental is hugely popular but the holiday letting market is relatively small.
- Some popular tourist destinations such as the Dordogne, Lot

21

and Tarn have a large stock of holiday property but support a comparatively modest long-term letting market.

Making the Right Choice

Within a fairly narrow price band a range of properties is clearly defined by the four categories above. Each has its own attractions and disadvantages so it is important that the buyer has a clear perception of what his requirements are.

Nothing is more likely to bring a look of despair onto a French estate agent's face more quickly than being given no guidance beyond price. In the UK the motto may well be 'you pay your money and take your choice'. For the French it is the other way around.

THE REGIONS

Some prospective buyers may already have homed in on a geographical target area, others may prefer to begin by investigating the relative merits of different regions. The prices under each entry in the table below indicate a typical T3 apartment, the first entry being purchase price and the second a monthly rental.

Table 2.4 Purchase price and monthly rental in different regions

The Pas de Calais and the coastal strip of Picardie around Boulogne and Le Touquet	Boulogne	
	€110,000	€ 1,050
Normandy, particularly around Deauville and Honfleur	Cabourg	
	€ 94,000	€ 835
Brittany, especially the coastal strips between St Malo & Roscoff, Quimper and Vannes	Lannion	
	€135,000	€395

The Loire valley in general, but mainly around Tours and Blois	Tours	
	€87,000	€500
Charente and Charente Maritime	Royan	
	€105,000	€575
Paris	Montmartre	
	€205,000	€1,050
The Dordogne and Lot	Cahors	
	€177,000	€665
Gironde	Bordeaux	
	€155,000	€600
Provence in general but especially the Vaucluse and the areas around Nimes and Aix-en-Provence	Aix-en-Provence	
	€160,000	€895
Burgundy	Dijon	
	€88,000	€495
Vosges	Epinal	
	€95,000	€575
Languedoc	Montpellier	
	€120,000	€800

The inconsistency of these prices, particularly with regard to rental values, reflects the difficulty in assessing the market. The above prices were quoted by accredited Fédération Nationale des Agents Immobliers (FNAIM) agents in November 2004, but only the barest details of the condition and precise location of each property were given. In each case the rental prices were for long-term lets (six months or more) but much higher returns could be achieved, particularly during the season, on a holiday rental basis.

Figure 2.1 Regional hotspots

Target areas

Buyers of French property to rent need to assess their target area carefully. It is surprising that many prospective buyers do not investigate the merits of different parts of France. Each region has its own character and each scores differently on a checklist of advantages and disadvantages.

Invariably, rural areas provide the greatest bargains. These are generally the parts of France where agriculture once bloomed and the population rose rapidly during the last two centuries. More recent and ever-increasing industrialisation has pushed this population trend into reverse and has created an over-supply of country properties. At the end of 2004, best value buys were in the Limousin, the Ardèche, Haute Vienne, Cantal, Les Landes and Nevers. But whilst each of these areas has its merits and may provide a satisfactory return in terms of long-term rental arrangements, they are rarely included on tourist itineraries.

Target pointers

Ask yourself what your priorities are. Remember that it may be harder, in theory, to 'sell' a remote location but, at the same time, lower property values may enable you to finance the kind of development (perhaps with the addition of a swimming pool) that makes the property more desirable to family groups looking for a 'chill out' holiday.

Try listing these considerations in your own order of preference:

- Easy access by car
- Facilities such as a swimming pool and barbecue on site
- Proximity to local shops and services
- Climate warm and sunny all year round
- Cultural and historical opportunities nearby
- Close to a beach
- Close to rail and air links
- Area particularly suitable for children
- Area appropriate for specialist hobbies and interests, e.g. golf, fishing.

If you plan to use the property yourself, these preferences are paramount. It can also be argued that, even if you hope to let the property all the year round, your marketing may be more positive if you are entirely enthusiastic about what you have to offer.

The Tourist attraction factor

There can be no doubt that certain popular tourist attractions affect the short-term letting market in particular. Sometimes these defy the seasons – Paris is popular all year round not least because of the proximity of Euro Disney: Futuroscope has made Poitiers another year-round destination.

Other attractions are less obvious. The Orne Valley has become popular for winter white-water canoeing; the Jura is popular with winter cycle tourists. The French themselves never undersell any tourist attraction. Some of these are well known, others less so. In recent years; the French themselves have begun to discover the following regions:

- *Aquitaine:* The 'new Loire'. Those who find the draw of châteaux and their gardens irresistible.
- *The Auvergne:* The upper reaches, in particular around les Mondeux, have become popular with those who prefer a slightly more *'tranquille'* ski experience.
- *Franche-Comté:* An increasingly popular summer location which features two superb forests (Forêt de La Joux, Forêt de La Fresse) a classic view point (Pic de L'aigle) and the much-photographed Lac de Chalain.
- *Poitou-Charentes:* This area, after the Côte d'Azur, has the greatest concentration of French holiday homes. The old town of La Rochelle attracts large visitor numbers particularly in the summer; Saintes is charming, elegant and steeped in history; La Palmyre is the best zoo in Europe; and the beaches around Royan are perhaps the finest in France.

Consider which region of France best fits the profile of your budget and personal preferences. The following thumbnail descriptions may help:

The Pas de Calais and Picardie

Most visitors see only the less attractive areas around the ports of Calais and Dunkirk from the autoroute. Of all the French regions though, this is the one with the greatest intensity of British-owned property. The advantageous price differential was somewhat eroded when the British property market declined

alongside the value of the pound in the late 1980s.
Although not obviously attractive to visitors, there are some
'undiscovered' gems – such as Montreuil-sur-Mer and the
delightful Poix de Picardie. There is, however, little activity in
the long-term letting market and this has traditionally been an
area largely ignored by tourists.

ADVANTAGES Transport links* Easy access* Reasonable prices*
THE DOWNSIDE Weather* Poor letting potential* Plain
              countryside*
'BUY TO LET' RATING Only deluxe facilities will attract
              holidaymakers

Normandy

There is good access to the UK through Caen, Cherbourg, and
Le Hâvre. In the late 1990s bargains were picked up by the
British, particularly around Honfleur and Deauville.
Consequently, local builders earned a good living renovating
inexpensive cottages. The situation has changed recently but
there are still bargains to be had, particularly in larger rural
properties.

Coastal property is relatively expensive, particularly around
Ouistreham, Trouville and Deauville. There are better bargains
to be had on the Cotentin peninsular. Inland and to the south
there are still bargains to be had in the area known as Petit
Suisse (particularly around Clécy) in the Orne valley. Prices
generally increase towards those areas accessible from Paris for
a weekend retreat.

ADVANTAGES Rolling countryside* Half-timbered houses*
              Access*
THE DOWNSIDE Few coastal bargains* English weather*
'BUY TO LET' RATING Take care but there are still exciting
              possibilities

Brittany

Brittany is more difficult to access but it remains justifiably popular with British buyers. The influence of the Gulf Stream makes part of the coast – especially in the north and west – remarkably mild for the latitude. The area around St Malo, Dinard and Dinan is delightful but prices reflect this. There are better bargains to be had along the coast westwards towards Roscoff where there are some sheltered gems of seaside villages such as St Jacut de la Mer. It should be remembered that the western Brittany peninsular (Finistère) suffers the worst of the winter Atlantic gales and that towns such as Brest and Quimper are nearly as distant from the Channel ports as the south of France. The southern parts of Brittany and Loire Atlantique are more accessible and have an even milder winter climate. The coastal strip from La Baule through St Nazaire and across the Loire estuary to Pornic is particularly popular with the French themselves for second homes. Letting values here are considered to be a good return on property investment, although holiday letting is restricted to a relatively short season.

ADVANTAGES Dramatic coastline* Seafood* Breton culture*
THE DOWNSIDE Atlantic gales* Impossible to remember place-names*
'BUY TO LET' RATING Some real possibilities but location is everything

The Loire Valley

The Loire river is said to be a major climatic division. It is certainly true to say that during the summer months the influence of the *Midi* (the south) is noticeable.

The Loire valley is also the market garden of France. It is an area rich in history and is very much on the tourist itinerary. Routes to the Loire from Channel ports are not good, but the projected motorway link from Alençon to Rouen will improve matters. Some popular centres such as Saumur and Amboise have become hugely popular with the British. The French themselves have a high regard for Tours. Prices reflect these preferences, but there are some delightful small towns where the 'buy to let' equation is more favourable. These include Loches, Montrichard, Chinon, La Flèche and Ingrandes.

ADVANTAGES Steeped in history* Iridescent light* Classy towns*
THE DOWNSIDE On the US tourist trail* Winter woollies required*
'BUY TO LET' RATING Some real potential here but the season is short

Champagne-Ardennes

The area has two distinctive characters – the upland forests of the Ardennes and the undulating chalk-fields of Champagne. There are some lovely villages and pleasant walled towns – such as Langres and Leon. Property prices are competitive and the area is almost undiscovered by the British.

ADVANTAGES Access to northern Europe* Some bargain properties*
THE DOWNSIDE Modest letting potential* Wet winters*
'BUY TO LET' POTENTIAL Only if you find a real bargain

Charente and Charente Maritime

This area has opened up recently because of improved motorway links. Unfortunately, this means it has become increasingly popular with British buyers. In the more rural areas, however, there is still a plentiful supply of relatively inexpensive property and the area is, therefore, worth considering for those with a limited budget.

The area around Cognac and Saintes attracts the majority of

inland buyers, whilst properties in the (more expensive) fishing ports and holiday towns and islands to the northwest are frequently the choice of seasonal visitors. The area bordering on the Limousin, immediately north-west of Angoulême (around Ruffec), represents excellent value, although the (short) winters can be bitterly cold. Indeed, temperatures in recent years have fallen to –16°C.

ADVANTAGES Inexpensive property* Best sunbathing coast in France*
THE DOWNSIDE Wet and windy winter* Becoming popular with Brits*
'BUY TO LET' POTENTIAL Well worth considering

Midi-Pyrennees

This is a massive area, comprising the French sector of the Pyrennees, the south-western corner of the Massif Central and the long valley in between. Toulouse, astride the Canal du Midi and Garonne, is the natural capital of the region.

The Pyrennees, still regarded by some as Europe's final frontier, has been massively developed for snow sports and climbing. There are few property bargains here. Toulouse itself is fairly pricey, and properties on the coastal strip around Perpignan and Argelès sur Mer are around twice the price of those encountered on the nearby (Spanish) Costa Brava.

ADVANTAGES Good year-round coastal climate* Real letting potential*
THE DOWNSIDE Fairly pricey property* Long distance by road*
'BUY TO LET' POTENTIAL Possibly just not good enough at these prices

The Limousin and Auvergne

Known as 'La France Profonde' (deep France), the Auvergne

has also been described as France's 'Wild West'. The volcanic landscape is breathtaking, with villages, such as Orcival, rivalling any in the country for character. Winter woollies are required, but it may be worth it for the best value (and cheapest) property in France. The improved motorway links have made the Auvergne a recent target for bargain hunters, but this is a thinly populated area so the buyer may find himself exploring far from the beaten track.

The Limousin has lakes, gorges, forests. For *la vie tranquille* it scores at the top of the scale. And its colourful capital, Limoges, is steeped in history. As with the Auvergne, prices are low but beginning to climb gently as the British discover it.

ADVANTAGES Rural beauty and solitude* Best bargains in property*

THE DOWNSIDE Letting potential patchy*Access* Short sharp winters*

'BUY TO LET' POTENTIAL A real gamble but the stakes are smaller

The Dordogne and Lot Valleys

The Dordogne is one of France's longest and most beautiful rivers. The most attractive area between Bort-les-Orgues and Beaulieu-sur-Dordogne is also the most expensive. Better value can be had closer to the Lot. The Dordogne was one of the first areas in France to attract significant numbers of UK buyers. The area is now home to second and third generation Brits with a predominance of ex-academics and ex-military, often recognisable by their vintage Panama hats and similarly battered Volvos. The Dordogne Ladies Club and the Dordogne Organisation of Gentlemen (DOGS) each have their own committees, with rules carefully framed to avoid using the word 'class'. This should be taken as a clear signal to the 'wrong sort of people' that they simply do not belong here. The summer cricket festival at Eymet is the highlight of the social calendar.

The Dordogne is also the cauldron of France. Its high summer temperatures and humidity are either attractive or unbearable, depending on your preferences. The upper reaches of the region (towards the Auvergne) offer a more temperate summer climate. The Lot valley is arguably more promising in terms of 'buy to let' value. The area around Cahors in particular is well worth considering, and values are certain to increase when the west-east motorway link from Perigueux to Clermont Ferrand is complete.

ADVANTAGES Pleasant all-year climate* Best markets in France*
THE DOWNSIDE Fairly pricey* Try parking in August*
'BUY TO LET' POTENTIAL Almost as safe as houses if you buy sensibly. The facilities are as important as location.

Gascony

This ancient duchy, later part of Aquitaine and hence formerly the birthright of British kings, has recently become fashionable for Brits wishing to set up home in France. Following steeply rising property prices in the Dordogne and Languedoc, Gascony is fast becoming the latest enclave of ex-patriot Brits.

The coast, from Bordeaux to Biarritz, is virtually one flat sandy beach which offers the best surfing in Europe. Indeed, that same beach begins geographically as far north as Soulac (near Royan) and runs, almost without interruption, to the Spanish border at Hendaye Plage.

In contrast, inland, there are miles and miles of forest all virtually empty. The northern part of the territory is wine country – including such famous names as the Chaˆteaux Latour, Chaˆteaux Lafitte and Chaˆteaux d'Yquem. To the south are the foothills of the Pyrenees and Basque country.

The climate is generally mild and frost free in winter. Even the summer heat is tempered by Atlantic breezes. That part of the coast known as Les Landes seems uninhabited other than by mosquitoes with vampire instincts. Properties between Biarritz and the Spanish border are much sought after and consequently expensive. The best bargains are to be had along the corridor of the N134 between Roquefort and Pau.

ADVANTAGES Biarritz in June* Red wines* Spanish neighbours*
THE DOWNSIDE Mosquitoes* Biarritz in August* Spanish
neighbours*
'BUY TO LET' POTENTIAL Only in the right location at the right
price

Inland Provence

Good motorway links have made the area accessible. The climate is good all year round, apart from the few weeks when the Mistral blows down the Rhône valley. Even before Peter Mayle, Provence was a popular choice with British buyers. Property prices reflect this, particularly in the Vaucluse and around Nîmes and Aix-en-Provence.

Although this is not an area for the bargain hunter, it could still be regarded as value for money for buyers considering year-round lettings. Best value (again according to FNAIM figures) can be had around Ales, Vaison-la-Romaine, Bollène and Pont-St-Esprit.

ADVANTAGES Lavender breezes* Steeped in history* Climate*
THE DOWNSIDE The mistral* Prices* UK enclaves* Peter
Mayle*
'BUY TO LET' POTENTIAL Return on investment may not be
enough

The Côte D'Azur

The Côte d'Azur has been the summer playground for wealthy Brits for more than a century. Villas on the Cap d'Antibes appear to be reserved for minor royalty, geriatric pop stars and lottery winners. A modest apartment at Cagnes sur Mer is rather more affordable and will still have letting potential. As you go westwards, the towns become less fashionable and property is consequently cheaper.

ADVANTAGES* Hot dry summers* Excellent beaches* Air
      access*
THE DOWNSIDE Warm wet winters* Known as 'the coast of
      crime'*
'BUY TO LET' POTENTIAL Worth considering despite the prices

Burgundy

Burgundy offers fine wines and gourmet cuisine. It is a land of rich pastures and golden villages, which makes it both picturesque and pricey. Burgundy also has a network of navigable waterways, little used commercially, but ideal for messing about in boats. Thanks to the limited inroads that tourism has made into the region, there may still be some property bargains, particularly in the upland area, the Jura, which is known as 'old France'. Prices increase with proximity to the Swiss border.

ADVANTAGES Almost unspoilt* Picture postcard scenery*
THE DOWNSIDE Becoming pricey* Long winters*
'BUY TO LET' POTENTIAL Prices perhaps just a touch too much

The Vosges

The Vosges region again reflects the huge variety of what France can offer the property buyer. Although interest in this hilly and wooded region has increased in recent years, there are still bargains to be had. Delightful villages such as Bussang, Ferrette, La Hohwald, St. Amorin and Schirmeck vie for the attention of the buyer with the popular larger resort town of Masevaux and Plombières les Bains.

The Vosges is particularly popular with nature lovers and walkers who enjoy peace and unspoilt countryside. The names of towns and villages in the region indicate the historic links with Germany, and this is reflected in the local wine and food. In terms of 'buy to let', the Vosges is becoming increasingly popular as a winter location, although the road infrastructure is by no means as good as the Alps.

Although property prices are above average, the letting potential is quite good.

ADVANTAGES Some bargain properties* Germanic style and
tradition*
THE DOWNSIDE The roads in winter* Summer midges* Poor
access*
'BUY TO LET' POTENTIAL A possible winner for a moderate
outlay

The Rhone Alps

The area, which lies between Lyon and the Swiss border, is popular for both winter and summer sports. The summer weather is less certain than in the far south but is generally good. The snow-capped mountains tell you all you need to know about the winters. Holiday-letting potential is excellent, but property bargains are scarce.

ADVANTAGES Excellent letting potential* Year round postcard
views*
THE DOWNSIDE Winter access problems* Expensive property*
'BUY TO LET' POTENTIAL Good, but can you find the right
property?

Languedoc

The Languedoc has arguably the best climate in France, which may begin to explain why, for the British, the Languedoc is the new Dordogne. This hot-spot status has encouraged prices to rise rapidly, with agents claiming a near 30% increase in them years 2001/2002. This acceleration of values has not been maintained. Carcassonne (known as Corkassonnay by some of the British contingent) has become so popular that, despite the proximity of airports at Toulouse and Perpignan, it is now also accessed by scheduled flights. Prices in the more popular corners of Languedoc are as high as anywhere in France and outside Paris.

The Languedoc has also attracted buyers who have been 'pushed' along the Côte d'Azur by property prices. You will pay a premium in seaside towns like Narbonne-Plage, but there are still relative bargains to be had in and around Montpellier.

ADVANTAGES Climate and culture* Access by air* Montpellier*
THE DOWNSIDE Some pricey property* The British contingent*
'BUY TO LET' POTENTIAL Well worth considering despite the
Brits

Paris

Purchasers should, for instance, generally avoid the suburbs and take care when purchasing in the ninth *arrondissement*. But get it right in Paris and 'buy to let ' can be a winner. Only the most desirable apartments on the Mediterranean coast and luxury chalet-style apartments in the Alps produce such excellent returns, and in both those cases the initial investment is likely to be considerably greater. A 50 square metre apartment would cost typically around €165,000 and could quite realistically return €1,600 net per month.

The ninth *arrondissement* includes Montmartre and the Pigalle, which needs to be interpreted on a street-by-street basis in order to determine whether the area is 'chic' or 'colourful'.

Purchasers should also consider whether their tenants would be happy to lug their bags to the 12th floor flat in an apartment building where the lift is regularly out of use. As both driving and parking in Paris are the stuff of nightmares, close access to the metro and bus routes is very important.

ADVANTAGES Paris in the spring* High letting values*
THE DOWNSIDE Paris in the winter* Parking at any time*
'BUY TO LET' POTENTIAL Excellent return possible but take care

Corsica

France in the Mediterranean. The island has almost 600 miles of virgin coastline and a mountain interior rising to 9,000 feet. It is, for a few discerning Britons, the place to be.

Despite a reputation for lawlessness there is, in fact, less crime than in most of mainland France. And there is even what some locals call 'the bandit bonus'. This flows from the fact that nationalist and separatist groups have pretty much seen off big business. There are no condo complexes or time share high rises.

But you have to respect local traditions (bringing in a builder from the mainland is a big 'no no') and you have to speak the language. And because there is little property development per se it is difficult to buy property suitable for development. Property is not cheap either – although far less than the Côte D'Azur – and obtaining planning permission can be tricky. Access can also be a problem in the winter months.

ADVANTAGES Good letting returns* Discerning customers*
THE DOWNSIDE Poor out of season access* Planning
              restrictions*
'BUY TO LET' POTENTIAL Pretty good if you can find a suitable
             property

3

Turning Property into Profit

There are more ways of turning French property into profit than are sometimes considered. A short list could include:

- a hotel
- a *gîte*
- a long-term tenant
- a guesthouse
- time-share
- sub-letting or part-letting
- mobile homes
- campsite ownership
- *colonie de vacances.*

We shall take each of these in turn.

THE HOTEL

This is not an option usually considered by the UK buyer. Perhaps this comes largely from the perception that the French will inevitably do things better, and, that starting from a position of 'inferiority' is not a recipe for business success. On a large scale this may be true, but there are some very successful UK-owned hotel enterprises in France. However, it may also be true to say that these are the exceptions which prove the rule. Certainly, the hotel business is not for the faint-hearted, work-shy or inexperienced. But those who have had relevant experience in the UK have little to fear. Purchase of the business and cost thresholds are generally lower in France, and the most essential ingredient for success – expert help – is readily available.

Hotels in France generally charge about half as much for a room as you would expect to pay in the UK for two people sharing. A small hotel, particularly in some rural areas, can be less expensive to acquire than a gite.

Hotel accommodation is promoted by the local *syndicat d'initiative* – the French equivalent of the tourist information office.

THE GUESTHOUSE

There is no legal distinction between the hotel and guesthouse. In France they are all 'hotels'. The 'star' grading of accommodation is, however, a clear indication of what the visitor can expect. Only the most modest establishments do not provide ensuite facilities. Each room is priced according to its size, the number of beds, the extent of ensuite facilities and whether or not it has a 'view'. Breakfast is never included in the accommodation charge, and at peak periods even the most modest establishments will make it clear to prospective guests that the taking of an evening meal in the establishment is a 'condition' of letting a room. Some will also insist on a number of nights to be pre-booked and the 'week' is likely to run from Saturday to Saturday.

THE *GITE*

The word '*gîte*' simply means a holiday property to let. French *gîtes* are advertised in national UK newspapers, travel agents and via the internet.

The majority of *gîtes* are classed as '*gîtes ruraux*'. The designation *gîtes ruraux* is awarded by *Gîtes de France*. These are apartments or houses available for holiday letting situated in agricultural areas. To qualify, the property must be available for rental for a minimum of three months a year and the owner should live in the neighbourhood. One advantage of letting as a *'gîte rural'* is that the tax bill is lower than that paid by the owners of bed and breakfast establishments and guesthouses.

LONG-TERM LETTING

French law makes a significant distinction between furnished and unfurnished letting. The law of July 1989 requires that unfurnished accommodation must be let for a minimum of three years where the landlord is a private individual and for the minimum of six years where the landlord is, in effect, a company. Only when the landlord is a private individual is he entitled to insert a clause that will enable him to take the property back for business or family reasons.

Most people in the 'buy to let' market prefer to rent their property furnished. The conditions here come within the basic provisions of the French Civil Code. The landlord, however, has to deliver the property in a good state of repair and is responsible for most repairs. The tenant is responsible (article 1754 of the Code) for repairs to fireplaces, fire backs, window casings, mantelpieces, plaster work, floor stones and floor tiles where only some are broken, windows except when broken by hail, doors, casements, hinges, bolts and locks.

The tenant can sublet unless this is prohibited by the tenancy agreement. The tenancy agreement is made in writing for a fixed term and it comes to the end on expiry of the term, without the requirement of notice. However, if the tenant remains in occupation, it is assumed that he wishes to continue under the same terms and conditions. In order to get him out, the landlord requires a court order which will not take effect for two months. And, the court will often permit the tenant to remain for a further three months to avoid him suffering 'hardship'.

MOBILE HOMES

As in the UK, this is a market to approach with caution. The quality of mobile homes and chalets is variable from the almost sublime – large chalets with three/four bedrooms, two bathrooms and pleasant living areas costing up to €200,000, to a cheap and cheerful second-hand three by eight metre aluminium box. Largely because of lower property values, the market for mobile homes in France is smaller than that in the UK. Most are seasonal and are incorporated within campsites which also have facilities for touring caravanners and campers. Cheaper mobile homes have a letting life span of three to five years because of the deterioration to the interior caused by holiday usage. For those considering letting a mobile home, this depreciation needs to be factored into the profit and loss account.

Some site owners forbid sub-letting altogether, but others take the view that this is part of their business and can be only arranged through them. In many cases, the local authority determines the number of weeks that the site can be open.

There is also a distinction to be made here between holiday and residential sites, and holiday and residential caravans. In general, holiday vans are constructed for their seasonal purpose. This means, for instance, that they are not fully 'winterised'. On the positive side, the sites are most frequently in pleasant locations that are entirely suitable for their purpose. Residential vans – also called 'trailers' or 'mobile homes' – are built to four-seasons standard, and, subject to local authority approval, can be inhabited all the year round. The sites, however, are most frequently found on the fringes of urban conurbations on 'brown field' or reclaimed land. These vans may be relatively inexpensive to own but are rarely suitable for letting. There are, however, a few notable exceptions to this. Local tourism offices can supply the details. Alternatively try **www.campingfrance.com** – a site guaranteed to tell you more than you ever need to know about sites. The Internet section (p. 155) features a splendid 'geographical search'.

Ultimately, however, there can be no sector of the 'buy to let' market which is more likely to end in disappointment.

41

Statistically, mobile homes change hands at least twice as frequently as any other 'property' and the sites themselves change hands almost as regularly. It is possibly prudent to take the view that the only people likely to be successful in this market sector are those doing it on the scale of holiday park owners.

TIMESHARE

Bi-propriété

Whilst the semi-detached house is a British institution, *bi-propriété* is characteristically French.

The French own more second homes pro rata than any other nation in Europe. The *bi-propriété* boom began to decline a generation ago. Its popularity was based on a simple financial formula that provided substantial holiday residences for large families. Typically, two senior family members would buy a seaside or country house and share the use of it.

The right to enjoy this property was technically divided over two six-month periods. The responsibilities of each of the 'share holders' (co-owners) were set out in a contract.

The arrangement worked well in most cases through family co-operation and informal flexibility. During the summer months, extended large family groups would often get together. These half shares in the property were passed from one generation to the next.

Small families are more independent and generally require less spacious accommodation. The second home is now more likely to be a seaside apartment or condominium – much less suitable for a *bi-propriété* arrangement.

Bi-propriété left behind it a legacy of difficulties created when shares in the property are passed beyond the family. The share value of one half of a *bi-propriété* is worth only about 40% of the whole property's value.

Multi-propriété

What we in the UK call timeshare, the French call *multi-propriété*. There are some possibilities in sub-letting timeshare accommodation. This depends initially on three factors :

● the location of the apartments
● the weeks purchased
● paying below the market price for timeshare resales (normally achieved by 'bulk-buying' unsold weeks).

Even if you get the right apartments at the right price, time and place, there remain difficulties. These begin with the French definition of *multi-propriété*.

In general terms, *multi-propriété* is akin to the kind of operation that has confronted UK visitors to Spain and the Canary Islands. In France too, visitors are seduced by the promise of free holidays (and/or champagne) into a half hour 'presentation' (which is stage-managed over three hours) with the intention of persuading you to 'sign on the line'. In recent years, so many timeshare sharks have been caught in the legal net that most survivors have moved on to Holiday Club scams. On the positive side, it can be argued that timeshare traders have put their house (and apartments) in order. But, in France at least, timeshare still gets a rotten press.

The variety of terms used to describe it begins to explain why. Even France's finest legal minds have become confused about the legal status of some timeshare agreements. Although we may regard it as a long-term rental agreement for a particular property (normally a designated apartment), the word *propriété* means ownership.

This is stressed by the marketing men. *Multi-propriété*, with subtle variations can become *inter-propriété*, *poly-propriété* and *pluri-propriété* and more recently, *multi-vacances* (literally many holidays). The *multi-vacances* formula also translated into Holiday Club sales. This is the thinnest wedge-end of 'timeshare' because the purchaser is buying little more than a schedule of pre-paid future holidays which may depend on the seller's future liquidity.

The problem is, therefore, defining exactly what is being bought. In theory, all *multi-propriété* owners purchase a *jouissance* – the right to occupy and enjoy a property at a designated time.

Others become part of a *société civile* – a company that holds voting shares in the property. This is intended to give them a say in the way the property is managed. In practice however, as timeshare owners may be scattered around a dozen countries, the management function is performed by an agent, whose decisions may sometimes seem totally arbitrary.

Multi-propriété has its afficionados, who claim it is a way of enjoying a holiday home at a modest price. The initial price of a timeshare week is generally between €8,000 and €12,000. Re-sale prices are invariably less than 40% of that.

There are, however, advantages. Timeshare apartments are often high quality, well maintained and may be exchanged (for an additional fee) for a similar timeshare in another location. But, before considering timeshare, ask yourself:

● How much does the contract really cost? Budget annually, and remember to count service, maintenance, and administration charges.
● Compare these figures to the rental of a comparable gîte for the same period.
● Is the purchase a sound investment? Marketing leaflets are likely to make this claim, but owners invariably lose money on re-sales. Pledges from timeshare companies to buy back at market price should be treated with suspicion. Remember it is even occasionally possible to 'acquire' free timeshare by simply taking over the existing owner's maintenance contract.
● What procedures are there for resolving disputes? Any multi-occupied building has potential problems. Timeshare, by its very nature, has more potential users than most.

- What rights do you have to sublet, or reassign your rights to others? Some timeshare contracts expressly forbid this. Problems can also occur with inherited timeshares, especially where there has been more than one signatory to an agreement.
- What are the arrangements for the maintenance of the building? Where timeshare purchasers are designated as co-owners, the ultimate responsibility is theirs not the management company's. A poorly maintained building will lose value rapidly and is more likely to be subject to vandalism.
- Are carpets, curtains, fixtures and fittings replaced systematically and regularly? There is evidence to suggest that equipment in multi-occupied apartments will wear out three times as quickly as usual. This means a life of one year for a bed mattress and no more than two years for a domestic quality carpet.

Despite many reservations, timeshare should not be discounted as a ' to let' opportunity. Tread carefully and there are bargains to be had. But the standing charge remains the *bête noire* of timeshare 'ownership'. These charges are often excessive and purchasers need to verify that the charge includes proper maintenance to the fabric of the apartment block and its grounds as well as to the apartment itself, and that these arrangements will continue.

There is invariably a trade off between service charges and the asking price of the timeshare weeks, with the service charge historically being seen as part of the developer's 'hidden profit'. And, if the service charges appear to be unusually low, it may be because the developers do not sustain a full maintenance programme. It should also be pointed out that overseas timeshares purchased through French companies may not be covered by the full protection of French law.

LIVING OVER THE SHOP

As in the UK, a single property can be divided into residential and commercial 'zones': this would most typically be a 'living over the shop' arrangement. This can present some difficulties in the 'buy to let' market for the following reasons:

● There will be separate, though inter-linked, contracts for the purchase of the business and the residential accommodation. These may be difficult to separate for the very good reason that the residential portion of the property is considered unsuitable for the use of anyone other than the business proprietor. Typically, he may have been a baker or butcher who commences work at three or four o'clock in the morning. In order to divide the contracts, it is necessary to prove that the accommodation to be let is not inter-dependent on, or could interfer with, the business. This, in turn, may mean providing a separate entrance(s) and/or sound proofing. Additional complications could arise if power and water supplies are combined.

● Different local and national tax regimes apply to business and domestic premises. If these have been combined for some time there are usually few difficulties; if, however, it is intended to separate them, responsibilities must be clearly defined.

TENANCY MANAGEMENT

If you buy premises in France that include a business which you do not wish to run yourself, you may wish to consider the possibility of letting it. But, if you grant a commercial lease for the business premises, it will run for nine years, on three-year rent reviews. At the end of the nine-year period, the tenant will have the right to renew, unless he receives the market value of the business plus his removal costs and the costs of purchasing an equivalent business.

But there is a possible way around this. You can put in an

independent manager as tenant of the business without granting him a lease. This relationship is called *location-gérance* (tenancy management). This special relationship provides that the tenancy management agreement must be registered at the Registry of Commerce and that for the first six months the owner of the business is jointly liable with the tenant for the debts. After that period, the tenant runs the business at his own risk and will pay an agreed rent.

CAMPSITES

There are more campsites in France than in any other European country. Visitors may have the impression that these are easy to set up and will do good business. Before entering this market, however, the potential buyer should be aware that :

- Only designated land can be used for campsites. Access and health and safety regulations are paramount, and the French authorities will take a dim view of any plan that has not been thought through.
- Most French campsites are owned by the municipality and either administered directly by them or under a franchise agreement. The intention is not primarily to make a profit from the site operations but to draw in visitor revenue. Local authorities sometimes take a jaundiced view of a would-be campsite operator who is going into direct competition with their own provision.
- Getting permission for a campsite operation, however, is not impossible. The simplest sites – *camping sauvage* – need provide only the most basic facilities. Camping *à la ferme* requires the provision of water points, showering facilities and toilets.
- The provision of campsite infrastructure is becoming increasingly sophisticated. Most sites now provide, for instance, electricity *branchements* and motor caravan service points. Maintenance and servicing of this equipment is,

however, expensive. The camping market is, therefore, not one to be entered without a considered business plan.

COLONIES DE VACANCES

Some UK buyers have successfully set up *colonies de vacances*. Here, facilities are provided for groups, usually of young people, to enjoy outdoor activities of various kinds. It is not unknown for land to be purchased, re-designated and let for this purpose. Although *colonies* are encouraged by the French authorities, health and safety standards are stringent. The qualifications of those planning this sort of operation will also be closely scrutinised.

4

Buying the Property

THE UK ESTATE AGENT

An increasingly large number of UK estate agents are represented in France. Most commonly these are 'piggyback' operations, where the UK agency is adjoined to a French agency. Some agencies, however, have associations with French agents as well as their own regional offices.

A few agencies, however, do things differently. They attract custom at UK-based exhibitions and 'profile' new customers before promising to find French property that suits the buyer's budget and personal preferences. They claim to provide a one-stop service intended to deal with every aspect of the purchase process.

But the process is not always as straightforward and transparent as the publicity suggests. Included in one 'package', for instance, is advice on rights of way, land divisions etc. The same agency even talk about *popping in for a cup of tea to see how you are getting along after the purchase*. They also encourage the view that a successful gîte or bed and breakfast business can be off and running within a few months, and that continued support and assistance will be available to help make this possible.

Prospective purchasers should be careful about these claims. On occasion, buyers have been brusquely informed, following the purchase, that continued agency expertise, or a referral to an appropriate professional, is indeed available – at €100 an hour. And, although their fee is 'all inclusive' (including legal work and taxes) 'one-stop services' do not come cheaply. One agent's scale of charges in 2004 ran from a minimum of €5,500. For the purchase of an €30,000 property in the Charente, in the same year, the agent's bill was €8,800. In effect, the purchaser paid twice the normal cost of the transaction process.

The buyer must decide for himself whether this kind of 'bells and frills' package is worth the premium rates charged. Judging by the dissatisfaction of some customers, it is certainly worth checking the small print. Communication throughout in English may seem like an advantage, but this assumes that French estate agents and lawyers are poor communicators. They are not.

It is also worth noting that matters such as 'rights of way' and 'land divisions', etc. are routinely checked by the lawyer handling the legal work, and that some other elements of the package – such as 'drawing up a will' – can be done separately and relatively inexpensively. It is also worth asking if it is realistic to think that you can turn a property – which could require some renovation – into a successful business within a few months.

And, if communication remains an issue, there is an excellent network of UK agents, offering the same services at the same scale of charges as their French colleagues. **www.real-estate-european-union.com** has definitive listings. You will also find valuable advice delivered with the voice of integrity and experience at **www.findaproperty.co.uk** and **www.hamptons-int.com**

THE FRENCH ESTATE AGENT

More than 50% of French properties are bought through French estate agents.

The *agent immobilier* is rather more respected in France than in the UK. This may partly be because the profession is highly regulated. Before he can set up in business, the agent must have:

- high standards of qualification, competence, and experience
- a professional permit to cover all property transactions – the permit has to be reviewed annually by the local *prefecture de police*

- professional indemnity insurance
- bank guarantees that cover him for all the money he holds on behalf of clients; it is illegal for him to hold cash if the guarantee is for less than €85,000
- up-to-date knowledge of the cost of transactions and market values: he is required by law to give this information and to give it honestly
- power of attorney (*mandat de vente*) before he may negotiate any sale on behalf of the vendor. The *mandat* has to be reviewed after three months; the agent may not purchase any property for himself for which he holds a *mandat* for sale
- specified rates of commission written into the power of attorney and prominently displayed in his office.

Payments to estate agents

In France it is, traditionally, the purchaser, rather than the vendor, who pays the agent's commission. This is no longer universally the case, however, as agents in some regions have adopted the more common EU practice of charging the vendor. It makes little difference in the end. The commission is hidden in the purchase price if the vendor pays for it; if a property seems unusually cheap it may be that commission is to be added.

Commission rates were once fixed by law but agents may now charge what they think the market can stand. In practice, they usually ask 5% (plus VAT at 18.6%), but the rate can be higher for upmarket properties.

THE *NOTAIRE*

The French solicitor, the *notaire*, is highly qualified and well respected.

- His authority is necessary to create valid contracts.

- His occupation is regulated by the Ministry of Justice and his professional association, the *Chambre de Notaires.*
- He is entitled to act (and usually does) for both parties in a property sale. This means that sales through a notaire's office are generally cheaper than those through an estate agent.
- He is obliged to explain impartially the implications of the clauses of contract.
- He is entitled to act as a sales negotiator.
- He is invariably employed to negotiate complex sales such as those that involve co-ownership, or after a death or divorce.
- He draws up the act of sale, verifies the vendor's right to sell, checks planning regulations, and notes existing charges against the property. Where these are greater than the sale price, he must ensure that the creditors can be paid in some other way.
- He is responsible for collecting registration fees and passing them onto the proper authorities.

PROPERTY PURCHASE CONTRACTS

A contract for the sale of property in France is more like the Scottish system than the English. Once a preliminary contract has been signed, it is both difficult and expensive to back out of the deal. One advantage of the system is that gazumping is almost unknown in France. Two forms of contract are in current use: the *compromis de vente* and the *promesse de vente.*

Compromis de vente

Signing the *compromis de vente* means that the vendor and purchaser are committed. It is possible to include 'get-out clauses' in the contract (*conditions suspensives*), but these usually relate to obtaining a mortgage and checking the authority to sell. You cannot, for instance, indicate that the purchase depends on finding a suitable tenant for the property or obtaining the required permissions to set up a *gîte* or bed and breakfast business.

Conditions suspensives take precedence over other clauses. If they cannot be fulfilled, the contract becomes null and void and deposits are returned.

The *compromis de vente* is the normal form of agreement in a private sale. The contract can include penalty clauses to be imposed by either the vendor or purchaser if the sale breaks down for any reason other than those listed in the *conditions suspensives*. The rest of the contract is a standard one.

The conditions of sale are clearly set out in the *compromis de vente*. These include:

- The responsibilities of vendor and purchaser
- Any easements that affect the property – such as public footpaths, naturally occurring water sources and any other parts of the property or its grounds which must be maintained as they are. This could include a designated area of woodland or a boundary wall
- Any government pre-emptive rights – such as water testing or special regional development projects
- The *conditions suspensives*
- The agreed price and method of payment.

A deposit is paid – normally 10% – on the signing of the *compromis de vente*. This is held by a third party (either the *agent immobilier* or the *notaire*) until final contracts are signed.

Properties are bought 'as seen' because owners are bound by law to reveal all defects they are aware of. Unfortunately, this is no guarantee that all is well. In the event of a problem arising after sale, the purchaser finds himself in the unenviable position of having to prove that the fault was likely to have been known before the signing of the *compromis de vente*.

The *promesse de vente*

This is a shortened version of the *compromis de vente*. Here, a type of completion is set against an agreed price and certain legal conditions and requirements.

Although the buyer has a period of time to 'reflect', he is still likely to lose his deposit if he pulls out of the deal. The main distinction is that the *'promesse'* is a unilateral agreement to sell, whereas the *'compromis'* is binding on both parties. Whichever agreement is signed, this leads to the *'acte authentique'*, which is the final conveyance of the property from seller to buyer.

The *acte authentique*

The *notaire* will draft a contract (*projet de l'acte*) a week or two before the completion date. This is sent out with a letter of convocation, which reminds both parties of the date agreed upon to sign the final agreement.

The *acte authentique* is essentially the same contract as the *compromis de vente*. Additionally it will:

- clearly identify the property and land
- provide a clear analysis of ownership rights for at least the previous 13 years; when the property is new this will refer to the ownership of the land
- refer to searches made and authorisations issued. These relate to planning regulations, easements and guarantees.

Power of attorney

French law requires both parties to be present at the signing of contracts. This could involve an English purchaser in extra journeys to France, unless he signs a *mandat* (power of attorney). This will give the *agent immobilier* or the *notaire* permission to sign contracts on his behalf.

Additional cost of purchase

There is perhaps no such thing as a typical transaction, because the *agent immobilier* may charge either the vendor or the purchaser. *Notaires*, however, charge on a scale of fees that relate to the agreed sale price. The following scale of charges is fairly typical:

First € 3,333 of purchase price – about 5%
From €3,334 to €6,666 – at 3.3%
From €6,667 to €18,333 – at 1.65%
Rest of purchase price – 0.85%

There are five additional fees payable when purchasing property. These arc again percentages of the property price:

- *taxe départmentale* – 4.2%
- *taxe communale* – 1.2%
- *taxe régionale* – typically about 1.2%
- stamp duty – 0.6%
- land transfer register – 0.1%

The following example is based on an agreed price of property of €100,000:

Table 4.1 Fees based on agreed property price of €100,000

Sliding scale legal fees:	
● For the first € 3333 (at 5%)	€ 166
● For the next € 3333 (at 3.3%)	€ 110
● For the next € 11,666 (at 1.65%)	€ 191
● For the balance € 81,666 (0.85%)	€ 693
● VAT on the above (at 18.6%)	€ 216
Registration fees	
● *Départementale* (at 4.2%)	€ 4200
● *Communale* (at 1.2%)	€ 1200
● *Régionale* (at 1.2%)	€ 1200
● *Hypotheqe* (at 0.1%)	€ 100
● Stamp duty (at 0.6%)	€ 600
● Total (at 8.7% of agreed property price)	€ 8676

These fees remain fixed, regardless of who negotiates the sale.

An *agent immobilier*'s fee is usually a flat rate of 5% (€5,000 in this example) so the total becomes € 13,676, or 13.68% of the property price.

If, on the other hand, the *notaire* negotiates the sale (acts as an *agent immobilier*) he charges a sliding scale for his services. Typically this would be:

For the first €29,166 (at 5%)	–	€1458
For the next €70,833 (at 2.5%)	–	€1770
Promesse de vente (at 0.3%)	–	€ 300
VAT on the above (at 18.6%)	–	€ 565
Total:		€4184

This alternative total becomes €12,860, or 12.86% of the property price. It will be noted that it is invariably cheaper to buy through a notaire.

INSTALMENT PURCHASE

This is a peculiar French arrangement, which may be advantageous to those 'buying to let'. It allows you to rent a property whilst also buying a proportion of the equity value. This process – which is called *location-vente* – has no exact parallel in English property transaction, although some housing associations offer a shared equity scheme. There are two methods of *location-vente*: the *promesse unilaterale de vente* and the *achete en viager*.

The promesse unilaterale de vente

The property developer or his agent lets a house or apartment in the normal way but included with the lease is a promise to sell – the *promesse unilaterale de vente*.

The tenant pays a higher rent than usual, which includes an element towards the agreed purchase price. An initial time period is fixed. This is generally two or three years. This method is offered by property developers when the market is slow. The main advantage to the tenant is that his payments will be lower than if he were repaying a mortgage. As with a mortgage, however, he will acquire only a modest equity (between three and five per cent) during the initial contract term. If he then decides to buy, this amount is, in effect, deducted from the purchase price. If the tenant decides against buying, he forfeits all the money he has paid.

The *achete en viager*

By this method the purchaser pays a substantial 'rent' for an indeterminate period of time before acquiring the property.

Again two contracts are combined. One is for the 'rent', and the other sets up an annuity with the vendor as the named beneficiary. This annuity is the *achete en viager*.

When the sales contract is drawn up, the property is valued. The annuity is determined on actuarial scales: the greater the vendor's life expectancy, the lower the annuity payments will be. This method is employed by specialist lawyers whose clients are elderly, and who have no dependent relatives or children. Entering into this type of contract is simply a gamble. The purchaser is effectively paying an income to the vendor in exchange for inheritance rights.

THE TIMESCALE OF PURCHASE

In the UK it is possible to complete or purchase formalities within six weeks. However, the process in France takes longer.

Prospective purchasers in the 'buy to let' market should also be aware that obtaining a mortgage may not be straightforward. Lenders begin by assuming that the property purchaser intends to live in the property. Although the problem is easily overcome, it is best to make this clear from the beginning.

COMPANY PROPERTY PURCHASE

It is possible to set up a company for the purpose of buying French property. The most commonly considered advantage of this is that company shares are not subject to French inheritance tax. There are, however, possible disadvantages with regard to capital gains and company taxes, and the need to claim tax exemptions before annual deadlines. The company may also need to appoint an agent and will certainly require the services of a French accountant.

BUYING OR BUILDING A PROPERTY UNDER CONSTRUCTION

In the UK, new properties sell at a premium. It is also true to say that having a house built for you or building it yourself, is generally the cheapest way of acquiring a property. These rules also apply in France.

Building land

The French divide land into zones – residential, artisanal and industrial. If land is identified on town plans as residential, then a domestic building is permitted as long as regulations are followed.

Planning permission

Planning permission (*permis de construire*) is not, as in Britain, permission to build. The right to build is implied when you buy building land – *terrain a bâtir*. This is because the land has been designated as suitable for domestic properties. However, permission is still required to erect a specific building on that specific site. If your property is from a *modèle* (a predetermined type, often from a 'catalogue'), planning permission is likely to be a formality and will take only two weeks to obtain.

Getting permission for building work sometimes appears to be no more difficult than taking photographs and drawing a rough sketch of what is required. This is then taken to the *mairie* where a clerk will fill in a form, and, about a week later, you will receive written approval. Every now and again, however, you will appear to fall foul of what appears to be a totally arbitrary rule. In some areas, if you live within 200 metres of an ancient church, you are not allowed to have green shutters. They have to be white or grey.

The cost of building

Most building is done through a development company. These companies invariably provide a range of *modèle* properties at attractive prices. The *modèles* have been designed to meet with planning regulations, and internal specifications can be negotiated. Many development companies have high street offices where sample 'packages' and prices are prominently displayed.

Base prices

The base price in September 2004 for typical *modèles* was:

- two bedroomed bungalow with garage of 80 m²   €50,000
- three-bedroomed bungalow with garage
  of 120 m²   €60,000
- four-bedroomed family house with garage
  of 180 m2   €100,000

Land prices

The cost of building land – *terrain de bâtir* – must be added to the base prices above. City and suburban land can be expensive, as can building plots with sea frontage. Elsewhere, building land usually costs between €30 and €35 per square metre. Land has barely risen in price over the last 20 years. In 2004, in some rural areas, it was still possible to buy land with outline planning permission for as little as €18 per square metre.

Designated building plots are usually about 500m² in larger towns and cities, between 500m² and 1000m² in coastal areas, and up to 2000m² in inland rural areas. A 750m² building plot may typically cost around €24,000 on the coast. The same money would buy a larger plot inland.

A 700m² plot could be approximately 35 metres long by 20 metres wide. A two-bedroomed bungalow, with a garage, or a three-bedroomed bungalow without a garage, or a four-bedroomed house with a garage, would have a floor area of 12 x 8 metres. These measurements would leave you with a garden area approximately the size of a tennis court.

The combined cost

A typical example of combining the house base price and land price was sampled in the town of Loches late in 2004. A 1000m² plot was available within the town itself for €15,000, and the same money could have bought a 2025m² plot in a village six kilometres away. The most popular *modèle* was a substantial three-bedroomed *pavilon* with a garage and a *sousl-sol*, fully carpeted and decorated with electric central heating. It was priced at €76,000.

Supplementary costs

The following is a checklist estimate of supplementary costs:

- connections for electricity and water   €2000
- local taxes and consent   €2950
- the *notaire's* fees for land purchase   €1170

Total costs

A breakdown of the total cost for the construction of a three-bedroomed bungalow in either of the locations mentioned above would break down as follows:

- purchase of land   €15,000
- construction of property (*modèle*)   €74,000
- connection of utilities   € 2,000
- local taxes and consents   € 2,950
- *notaire's* fees   € 1,170
- total cost: €95,120

For comparison purposes, the national index target price for a new (rural) development of similar specification is €127,000. The implication is that having a house built saves about 25% of the asking price of a finished property. It is a powerful incentive to build.

'Building packages' in France include allowances for fitted kitchens, bathroom suites and decoration. Gardens are also 'landscaped' as part of the deal, but this can mean little more than levelling the ground and removing rubble.

The building contract

The nature of this contract is defined by French law. It will include:

- a definition of what is to be built
- the quality standards required by the civil code
- the schedule of construction and associated work
- penalty clauses for the late completion by the builder or late payment by the purchaser

- information about the land, including access rights
- insurance required during the construction period
- the schedule of stage payments.

Building contracts are not standardised in the same way as those for lettings and normal house purchases. The time between signing a contract and occupying the property is normally around five months.

Stage payments

The building industry in France has suffered a mild recession in recent times. Prices are competitive and, in some cases, builders have cut profit margins. This is good news for the customer, but it also reflects vulnerability in the industry.

Standards in the construction industry are controlled and are normally high. The French do not have an equivalent expression for 'cowboy builder', which is reassuring, but some construction companies have a better reputation than others. Local research and advice can pay dividends.

Stage payments offer some protection to the customer if the builder goes bust, but if a second company is employed to complete work it will inevitably be more expensive. The normal pattern of stage payments is:

3% after planning permission and signing the contract
10% on completion of the foundations
20% on completion of the building shell
20% when water connections are complete
15% when electricity connections are complete
15% when heating and plumbing is operational
10% after landscaping work is complete
5% on completion of interior decoration
2% on the handing over of keys.

Do not part with hard cash until the building permit has been granted. Most developers seek permission to develop a number of properties on land they own, so a permit is not usually a problem, but it is the only guarantee you have that the building is legal. If it is not, the Government can demand that you return the land to its original condition. The risk is similar if the building does not comply with the authorisation, so make sure that the building you are having constructed is the same as the one in the permit. Modifications require a second building permit.

Both UK and French financial institutions are familiar with stage payments and loans can be phased accordingly.

Buying 'on plan'

Buying 'on plan' (*en état futur d'achèvement*), also confusingly known as 'buying off' plan, is a well-known purchase arrangement in France. It is certainly an option well worth considering. Many UK buyers, particularly those considering buying to let, are looking at apartments. The great advantage is that they are easy to maintain and easy to lock up and leave.

Late in 2004 there were new seaside apartements for sale at Vaux-Sur-Mer in Charente Maritime. One bedroomed-flats were were €69,000. Two bedroomed flats were €95,000. It was also possible to buy a one bedroomed flats at Vretignolles-Sur-Mer for €75,000. It was anticipated that the properties would be ready for occupation in the summer of 2005.

Buying a new property has financial advantages. These include·

- the ten-year buildings guarantee
- the two-year guarantee on fixtures and fittings
- reduced legal fees
- stamp duty and other costs on new properties which are between 2.5 and 3%, compared with 7% on properties more than five years old.

These apartments are often sold 12 months or more ahead of anticipated completion. Property in sought-after locations is often sold long before any of the apartments are completed. Prices may increase as each phase of the development is marketed and stage payments are applied.

It can work like this. Late in 2002 there were apartments – which included flats at Sainte Maxime in the South of France – due for completion in 2004. Prices starting at €120,000 Similarly, a property at Trouville in Normandy included two-bedroomed flats also due for completion in 2004 for €90,000. The area in which there has been the greatest demand for similar purchases is the French Alps. There, the incessant demand for property, combined with tighter planning controls, has accelerated prices. Despite traditional price stability, in certain very desirable locations, agents have claimed that property values have doubled in the last two years. Locations in the Alps are greatly sought after by 'buy to let' purchasers because of the income that they can generate all year round. It has been claimed by the Alpine Apartments Agency (**www.alpineapartments-agency.com**) that rental returns of eight to 10% annually are typical.

At the same time unsold flats in the second phase of the Residence des Alpes in Chamonix included apartments for completion late in 2003, with prices starting at €228,000. Rental potential from 'on plan' purchases is not confined to the Alps. Late in 2002 VEF (www.vefuk.com) marketed newlybuilt properties at La Rochelle from €160,000, and at Forntignan (near Mont Beligne) from €93,000. At the same time Az Assistanes (www.azassistanes.com) marketed newly-built property between Menton and Cannes. One-bedroomed apartments in attractive developments, with sea views, typically cost around €250,000. It is claimed that such properties can be let for €1000 a week in high season.

It could be argued that there are few bargains to be had for most of those seeking to purchase property in France when buying 'on plan', because developments are invariably on prime sites, often close to the sea, and finished to high standards. For those buying to let, however, the situation is rather different; because their target market is letting to people who want to be in such places, so returns can be correspondingly high. In some cases, the purchaser will see nothing more than plans and drawings. Developments are invariably phased and a second phase is likely to be an indication that the first has been successful. You should be suspicious if a development has been completed but a number of apartments remain unsold.

The 'on plan' contract

Contracts are fairly standardised:

- The particular apartment is identified and described and the price is fixed.
- The development schedule is explained.
- Rights and arrangements for co-propriete are set out as in laws of 1989.
- All stage payments and conditions of sale are set out.

Advantages of buying 'on plan'

'On plan' purchases are popular because:

- Buyers get a new property.
- Although 'on plan' apartments are at the pricier end of the market, the value of the finished apartment is sometimes greater than the *prix ferme* (the fixed price). Stage payments allow the developer to maintain his cash flow throughout the development process, rather than having to wait to sell the finished article. The purchaser, in turn, is rewarded for his act of faith (and sometimes his patience if poor weather slows the pace of development), by having the price fixed up to two years ahead of completion.
- When apartments are sold direct a *prix ferme* arrangement

often represents a small discount, as no estate agent is involved.

- The purchaser can inspect the property at various stages of development. He can choose his own scheme of decoration, colour of bathroom suite, style of kitchen units and appliances, and can even select floor tiles from a pre-determined range.
- Buyers can take advantage of stage payments by delaying loan applications, or by taking their time to dispose of other assets. Some hold cash reserves on deposit and arrange withdrawals in line with the payment schedule.
- Contracts rarely have severe penalty clauses for late payments. A month's grace is common, followed by a penalty charge of around 1% per calendar month.
- Contracts usually take six to eight weeks to complete but *notaires* can spin things out for longer than that.
- Banks and building societies are often less cautious about lending money 'on plan' than for other purchases. This is because equity values are easy to determine, developers are often large, successful (and solvent) companies, and the apartments are easily disposed of if repossession becomes necessary.
- Developers can often arrange attractive mortgage terms.
- Legal costs may be reduced if one *notaire* is used by the developer and a number of owners. This is because research time and paperwork is reduced and contracts can be drafted in blocks.
- Power of attorney (*mandat*), is often designated to third parties who will attend the *acte de vente* on behalf of the buyer. This power of attorney is not a short cut but a safeguard. A professional – familiar with French language and civil law – is more likely to make sense of the procedure and to identify last-minute problems. This can also save the purchaser time and money by making an additional journey from the UK unnecessary.

Spotting the sharks

Although 'on plan' purchases are generally satisfactory, some buyers have been disappointed or worse still, ripped off. Equally, some developers have claimed that it is the 'buy to renters' who are in fact the biggest sharks in the pool.

It is not unknown, however, for phantom developers to set up a mobile office (generally during the holiday season) and to take deposits for a project they have little or no intention of completing. At best this is testing the market; at worst it is fraud. Either way, it will be difficult to get your money back.

Legitimate developers go to great lengths to market their apartments. They produce well-drafted plans and glossy literature, and can generally point to a track record of success. If you are in any doubt ask around locally or check at the *mairie*.

Another 'dodge' can occur when a development is not selling as well as anticipated. The developer may decide to sell a few apartments to a third party at a reduced price. This third party (often a marketing company or estate agent) will then offer the apartments at slightly below the *prix ferme*. The purchaser buying through the third party finds mark-up fees added to the sale price. Later, the purchaser also finds himself paying the original developer for outstanding stage payments. This is legal and it can prove to be a bargain. In some cases, however, it suggests the developer was over-optimistic in forecasting profit margins and the resale value of the apartments could reflect this.

When an agent is selling several apartments in the same development, be suspicious. It may be that he has been appointed to sell all the apartments (in which case this should be declared), but it could also be an opportunist attempt to unload undesirable property or apartments which are less than favourably positioned or have poor views.

Doing it yourself

You can, of course, build your own house in France. Assuming the land you wish to buy is designated as building land, you will also need to ensure:

- Suitable access is provided.
- By-laws are complied with.
- You have a building permit, as required for a building that has a floor surface (*la surface hors d'oeuvre*) of more than 20 m², and for any external modification that changes the appearance of an existing building.
- The building must meet *co-efficient d'occupation des sols* (COS) guidelines. This is a splendidly complex formula that relates certain kinds of building to the amount of ground that can be built on within a designated zone. In essence, this means that in densely populated areas, the co-efficient may be one, meaning you can build on all the land. Elsewhere, the co-efficient will vary between 50% and 10%. At 50% you will require 200 m² of land to build a 100 m² bungalow; at 10% you will need 1000 m² of land for the same project.

Supplementary costs

When land is purchased, the services of a *notaire* are required. If a loan is needed for the acquisition of land, or for the property construction, fees will be charged for financial advice, for administration, and for registering the loan. The services of a surveyor (*géromètre*) are also required. Fees for this service are likely to be between €500 and €850.

The *compromis de vente* will contain a clause that makes the new landowner fence off his boundaries. The cost of this has recently been estimated at €20 a running metre. A typical plot of around 700 metres would therefore cost approximately €2200.

Getting the permit

La surface hors d'oeuvre is defined by the total ground area of a building. For buildings of more than one storey, all the storeys are added together, including attics and basements. *La surface* also includes the thickness of external walls, balconies and terraces.

The services of an architect (or a building company who employ an architect) are required for any building where *la surface* exceeds 170 m². Whilst many properties are below 170 m², this should not be seen as a licence to manage without professional backup. Specialised knowledge is required to draw up the required documentation for planning approval. This includes:

- a detailed site plan, including trees, existing outbuildings, boundaries and access
- a scale drawing of the proposed building, which includes all the elevations
- a complex form (PC 157), which must be completed and returned to the local *mairie*.
- notification of the hearing, at which all aspects of the proposed construction will be discussed. The application can be rejected on either architectural or environmental grounds.

Planning permission refused

If your plans are refused you have three options:

- to submit modified plans
- to accept any suggested modifications
- to appeal to the local administrative courts (*le tribunal administratif*) – this can be a very long process.

The secret of success is to talk informally to officials at the local *mairie* as you are preparing your plans. They know what is likely to be acceptable and what will be rejected out of hand.

Plans for improvements

Any changes to an existing property must also come within the *conseil d'orientation stratégique* (COS) guidelines. This means it is paramount to plan the totality of your development in advance. A plan may come well within COS guidelines but, if you subsequently choose to add a garage or a conservatory, you may find plans for these are rejected. As a rule of thumb, it is best not to consider any development which exceeds 44% of the total COS allowance. It may be that you have no wish to develop the property yourself, but the subsequent sale of the property could collapse when the prospective purchaser realises that he has no scope for development.

A declaration of intent (PC 156) must be signed and sent to the *mairie* by registered post. This must be accompanied by:

- a site plan
- listings of specification and materials
- plans of existing structures that will be modified or photographs with the modifications drawn in. Computer modelling is still not approved of by the planning authorities. This may be because it is relatively simple for software to be used to distort scale and distance, thus making the structures and/or their modifications 'appear' to fit within COS guidelines.

Buying at auction

UK buyers are generally suspicious about buying at auction (*ventes aux enchères*) but this remains a likely way of securing a bargain. Properties for auction are most frequently found in rural areas and are likely to be in need of renovation. There is unlikely to be a great deal of competition at the sale.

Many of these properties are the subject of inheritance disputes, intestacy or mortgage lenders' repossessions. The mortgage lenders are primarily interested in recovering their debt as swiftly as possible.

Details will be published six weeks before the sale in local newspapers. A standard form notes the place and the date of the sale, the lawyer who is handling it, the reserve price and arrangements for viewing. There is also a brief description of the property and its grounds.

Potential buyers, who are not required to attend the auction in person, appoint a lawyer registered with the *tribunal de grande instance* to make bids on their behalf. The lawyer seals bids – up to the maximum agreed – in envelopes.

At the close of the sale, the lawyer must deposit 10% of the purchase price. Other fees – amounting to approximately 20% of the purchase price – must be paid within a month. A judge presides over the auction itself. Two lights (equivalent to 'going once, going twice') are lit at the end of each round of bidding. A third light marks the 'winning' bid. In some rural areas the same procedure is still carried out in the more traditional way, with candles replacing the light bulbs.

Although this method of purchase may sound daunting, it is well worth considering if the property otherwise fits the bill. Renovated farm buildings make splendid *gîtes ruraux*.

5

Letting the Property

GÎTES

Gîtes provide furnished self-catering accommodation. They can be anything from a château to a farmhouse or a seaside apartment. They are classified according to facilities.

Holiday letting documentation

If you intend to run the business yourself, you will need to produce a 'letting pack' which includes :

- A written contract. This has to be signed by both parties and will include dates, the price and complete address of the let, and the name and the address of the proprietor and/or the letting agent.
- A detailed description of the property and its facilities. Each *gîte* is designated as suitable for a maximum number of guests. You should point out that if this number is exceeded you have the right to refuse entry to additional guests and/or to cancel the contract with immediate effect.
- A clear indication of the tariffs and supplementary costs. These may cover household linen, for example, as well as holiday taxes and indemnity insurance.
- A definition of the letting period. Traditionally, the French letting week runs from Saturday to Saturday. Some *gîte* owners also offer weekend bookings – usually two days and two nights, which invariably run from Friday evening to Sunday afternoon. Weekend lettings are not normally available during July and August.

- A statement as to the deposit required against damage and breakages. This will normally be set against an inventory, which is signed when the keys are exchanged.
- A clear statement as to the arrangements for cleaning. If a service is to be provided you should say how and when it will be available. If, however, cleaning is the responsibility of the guest(s) you should indicate this.
- A description of the arrangements for collecting and returning keys and for car parking.
- A statement as to the deposits required and the deadlines for payment.

France Magazine is a valuable source of advice to potential *gîte* owners. It also includes listing of quality *gîtes*, many of which are offered for the first time during the forthcoming season.

Advance payments for gîte accommodation

The deposit paid for a *gîte* is either an '*un accompte*' or '*arrhes*'. The legal distinction is important.

If the guest has paid an '*un accompte*', he can lose not only the deposit but the *gîte* owner can hold him responsible for the full amount due for the letting period. If the guest cancels having paid an *arrhes*, then only the deposit is forfeit.

However, this does not always mean that it is best to have the deposit described as an *arrhes*. *Un accompte* means the guest can make a claim for breach of contract if the *gîte* is unsatisfactory in some way or if he is denied access. Depending on these circumstances, the damages awarded could be considerable. *Arrhes*, under French law, means that the *gîte* owner is obliged only to pay twice the deposit he has received.

Tax incentives for *gîte* owners

There are tax incentives for owners who offer properties as *gîte* accommodation. In order to qualify, the *gîte* has to be available for at least three months of the year. It is not uncommon for the *gîte* owner to make the accommodation available only for the summer season. This is because he can obtain maximum revenue for the least inconvenience.

The right kind of contract

There are two basic types of contract:

- one relating to short-term 'holiday lettings'
- one relating to long-term leasing.

HOLIDAY LETTINGS

For holiday lettings the contract will look something like this:

> Holiday letting contract between Mrs. Holly Day Maker and Mr. Ivor Gite for self-catering holiday accommodation at La Maison D'Etre

This is subject to the following conditions:

1) This is a binding contract between the property owner (Mr. Ivor Gite), the nominated party leader, and every adult member of the holiday party.
2) A deposit of €100 is payable per week of the proposed holiday period, and this secures the agreed booking period. The balance of the rental is due not less than eight weeks prior to the start of the holiday unless late booking conditions have been agreed. Failure to pay the deposit in full will constitute a cancellation of the holiday by the holidaymaker. Reminders are not issued.
3) Cancellation of the booking by the holidaymaker should be made in writing. If the reason for the cancellation is illness, or other extreme unavoidable cause, the owner will repay,

excluding the deposit, the following amounts:

a. 29 to 56 days before holiday date – 50% of rental
b. 15 to 28 days before holiday date – 25% of rental
c. 0 to 14 days – 10% of rental
d. Where there is no qualifying reason for a refund, such as illness, no refund will be made. The owner of the accommodation will, however, allow deposits to be carried forward against suitable alternative holiday dates if these can be arranged.

4) The property owner is entitled to ask the holidaymaker to leave the property without any refund if in his/her opinion the behaviour of the holidaymaker and/or the holidaymaker's party is unacceptable.

5) Whilst every care is taken to provide an accurate description of the property, from time to time there may be alterations made. The holidaymaker must accept that no refunds are available for such discrepancies.

6) The property owner will endeavour to make sure the stated property is available for the dates contracted. In the event, however, for instance, of fire or flood damage, and the property therefore not being available, the owner will endeavour to find the holidaymaker a suitable alternative accommodation. If the cost of this alternative accommodation is higher, the owner will be jointly responsible with the holidaymaker for the price difference. If a suitable replacement property cannot be found, the holidaymaker is entitled to a full refund.

7) The number of persons using the property must not exceed the numbers agreed and the owner cannot accept more people than the maximum number advertised. If it is found that more people than agreed are using the property, this will be considered a breach of contract and the holidaymakers will be asked to leave immediately without any refund. Pets are allowed in the property subject to the property owner's agreement and that they have full certification as required in French law. The holidaymaker

should ascertain these requirements for himself. The property owner may require sight of such documentation. The type and numbers of pets must not exceed what is declared at the time of booking, otherwise a breach of contract will be deemed to have taken place. Holidaymakers are liable for all damage caused by their pets and are requested to remove all traces inside and out of pet occupation before leaving the property. A charge will be made for any additional cleaning required. Pets are not allowed on chairs, beds, or any other furniture or near play or swimming pool areas. Pets must at no time be left on their own in the holiday accommodation. The property owner is not responsible for any accident or injury occurring to a pet during the holiday period.

8) Arrival time should be no earlier than 15.00 on the start date and the holiday accommodation should be vacated by 10.00 on the departure date. It is the responsibility of the holidaymaker to arrange key collection at least 48 hours before the arrival date. The owner cannot be held responsible for any changes in travelling arrangements which are beyond his control.

9) The holidaymaker should keep the holiday property and all furniture, fittings and effects in the same state of repair and condition as at the commencement of the holiday. The property should also be left in the same state of cleanliness and general order in which it was found. The property owner will be entitled to make an additional charge if this is not the case. The holidaymaker will be responsible for all damage or loss of contents during the occupation and is also responsible for paying appropriate compensation to the property owner. Where holidaymakers abuse holiday property they will be responsible for making full restitution for the damage.

10) It is the owner's utmost concern that the holidaymaker has a pleasant stay. It is up to the holidaymaker to make any problem known to the owner immediately it becomes

apparent so that the owner has an opportunity to correct the situation. Unless this procedure is followed no claim can be accepted. It also must be accepted by the holidaymaker that there are times when professionals cannot immediately be found to rectify a problem. The owner will, however, do his best to rectify problems as soon as is reasonably possible.

11) Should the holidaymaker not wish to accept the above terms and conditions, he should write to the owner within two weeks of the deposit being paid in which case a full refund will be made. If such request is not made within two weeks it will be deemed that the holidaymaker has accepted the above terms and conditions.

LONG-TERM LETTING

Laws passed in 1986 and 1989 have been integrated into a standard contract (see appendices) which apply to all lettings of more than six months' duration. This clearly sets out all the rights and responsibilities of landlord and tenant.

The main points are:

- There must be a description of the premises and the equipment. This includes parking facilities and the arrangements made for maintaining gardens, intercoms, television antennae, hot and cold water systems, lifts, central heating, open spaces and the collection of refuse.
- Contracts are normally for three years initially. Any reason – such as family or professional – why this should not be the case must be clearly set out.
- Inspections of the property are annual and the date each year on which these will take place must be specified.
- The amount of the deposit, which will include an advance on rental, must be clearly specified.
- Where there is shared responsibility – such as the maintenance of the lifts and the open areas – the charges for these must be stated.

77

- Transaction fees and local fees in terms of setting up the rental agreement must be stated.
- Local charges and taxes of co-ownership must be specified.
- The tenant will sign for a particular number of keys.

The obligations of both landlord and tenant are also set out in the contract. These include:

- The tenant must give a minimum of three months' notice in writing. This can be reduced to one month in the case of loss of employment or of poor health of a tenant over 60.
- The owner must give a minimum of six months' notice in writing. This can be reduced only in the event of the tenant not carrying out his obligations.
- Six months before the end of the contract, the owner can propose renewals in writing either for less time (but a minimum of one year under the same conditions as previously) or for a minimum of three or six further years under conditions to be agreed.
- If the contract is for a period of less than one year (and this can only occur if the owner can prove family or professional reasons why this should be necessary) the reasons must be clearly given within the contract.
- For properties built before September 1948, a special clause deals with the general state of repair and maintenance and the minimum standards that must be maintained.
- The owner is permitted to recover from the tenant charges for repairs to equipment and services from which the tenant benefits. The owner must provide the tenant with a complete breakdown of these charges at least one month before they are due. All charges are to be fixed annually.
- The deposit may not exceed two months' rent and must be returned to the tenant not more than two months after the keys have been returned. The deposit can, however, be used to pay debts left by the tenant.

- Some improvements, where agreed by all parties and carried out by the owner, can lead to a modification of the rent payable.
- The owner's responsibilities include keeping the property in a good state of repair and keeping receipts for payments and charges.
- The tenant's responsibilities include making due rental payments, keeping the property in good order and permitting reasonable access by the owner or his agent at agreed times.
- A termination clause permits the owner to end the rental agreement following two months' non-payment of rent. The same clause also permits the owner to recover the cost of an expulsion order against a tenant.
- The tenant's obligations in terms of the conditions and consents required from the owner for sub-letting.
- Limitations applied to the use of the building. This is normally to prevent the tenant setting up, for instance, an art studio within a residential building.

Sub-letting

It is theoretically possible to let a property on a long-term basis and sub-let prime weeks – normally during the season for higher values. It should be pointed out, however, that long-term lease arrangements will contain legal clauses, the force of which will forbid sub-letting, although this is not to say that, with the landlord's permission, it is not possible to allow friends or family to use the accommodation.

Letting property under long-term letting agreements and holiday accommodation agreements comes under very different legal headings and is subject to different tax laws. Anyone benefiting financially, therefore, from sub-letting an apartment is entering a very grey area.

Legal protection of the tenant

Prospective purchasers of property to let should be aware that French law is said to favour the tenant over the landlord. Aspects of the lease confirm this view.

- The costs of setting up the lease agreement are shared between landlord and tenant. The rent review clause can only be exercised once annually.
- Any changes in the rent charged cannot be greater than the French government cost-of-construction index.
- Disputed claims about responsibility for maintenance and repairs are referred to an independent bailiff. His report is generally accepted by the court. This means that the landlord is invariably forced to carry out repairs.
- The tenant will normally have security of tenure for a minimum of three years. The only exception is the provision for repossession for family or professional reasons. Courts take a dim view of landlords who try to apply this clause unfairly.
- The tenant is required to give only three months' notice to quit. In the case of a person becoming unemployed or finding a new job, the requirement is limited to one month.
- If the landlord requires vacant possession, he must inform the tenant in writing six months before the expiry of the lease. If this does not occur, it is assumed that the lease will be renewed for a minimum period of a further three years.
- The tenant cannot be required to pay his rent by direct debit.
- The tenant cannot be required to make the property available for weekend inspections. Inspections, which must be subject to 'reasonable' notice, should not last more than two hours.
- The lease may have penalty clauses applied to non-payment of rent or service charges but not for the breach of any other obligation.

PRACTICAL TIPS

Although the long-term contract is standardised, the short-term (holiday letting) contracts are very varied. This can give rise to a number of problems:

- Who is responsible for light and heat? This is a particularly fraught point. In summer, these costs may be virtually non-existent and any charge would be seen as punitive. It is better, therefore, to include charges in the weekly letting fee and to make it clear that this is the case.
- Use of a swimming pool. This frequently unravels as an argument about a pool not being available, either because of maintenance, or for seasonal reasons. Again this should be made clear in the contract.
- Fuel for open fires and barbecues. A few logs by an open burning grate and a bag of charcoal or vine wood can obviate any 'misunderstandings' and help to provide a welcome for the visitors.
- Arrangements for cleaning the property and changing linen. Again, these should be specifically explained. Although, as in the above contract, it is not unusual for owners to require that the property is 'left as it is found', in practice this can be contentious.
- A welcome pack – perhaps containing some basic food stuffs and a bottle of wine should never be included as part of the contract. This can lead to disputes about what the pack could, or should, have contained. A welcome pack supplied, apparently gratis, however, helps to set the holiday mood and will form a favourable impression.
- Arrangements for the collection and return of keys should be made clear either in the contract itself or in an accompanying document. Nothing causes more problems for owners than travel-weary tenants who find that access to their holiday accommodation is temporarily denied.
- Whilst there should be reference in the contract to an

81

inventory, in practice this should be kept as brief as possible. A document which runs to ten or 12 pages and lists every item in the property is likely to provoke a negative response. The attitude of the holidaymaker is likely to be: 'Do you really think that I have travelled 600 miles to steal a corkscrew?'

FURNISHING AND FINISHING

In the 'buy to let market' the accent is on simplicity and utility. Quality furniture, furnishings and fittings in France are more expensive than in the UK. However, it is foolish not to do the job properly. Ask yourself the following questions:

- Are flimsy chairs and a cheaply veneered dining room table likely to stand the usage?
- When fixtures begin to look tatty are you likely to win return business?
- Renters look for much the same as they would in their own home. This includes easy-to-use appliances, sensible positioning of switches and plugs, doors and windows that open, close and lock easily, and plumbing which is discreet, quiet, and safe.
- Is a decorative scheme featuring shades of purple and green wallpaper, likely to appeal to the tastes of your paying guests?
- What kind of flooring is likely to have the greatest utility? Are stained boards and/or tiled floors (perhaps with a few discreet rugs) likely to look better and last longer than carpeting?

It is best to keep your fixtures and fittings within the vernacular of the building. If in doubt, keep things simple. White walls are never unfashionable. Large paved patios are easier to maintain than flower beds. A brick-built barbecue is a welcoming design feature and intrinsically much safer than its portable clip-together cousin. Always err on the side of the sensible and sturdy, and purchase items which are maintenance free.

GARAGING AND PARKING

Modern family houses and most rural properties will have garaging facilities – perhaps in the form of a *sous-sol* – included in the purchase price. However, where it is now often a requirement of development in the UK, garaging or private parking is not generally included in either the purchase or rental of an apartment or town house in France.

- A lock-up garage is likely to cost between €9,000 and €10,500 to buy.
- A permanent reserved parking space could cost between €3,300 and €7,500.
- An annual contract for secure covered parking could cost between €1,000 and €1,500.

A parking facility of some kind is essential. Not only is it difficult at certain times to find street parking in cities and popular resorts but it is worth recalling that France has the biggest incidence of theft of both vehicles and their contents in Europe.

PARIS LETTING AGENTS

Whilst letting agents are well established throughout France, the most complete services are offered in the capital. Some are specialists such as MFIP (**www.myflatinparis.com**), who can provide an end-to-end service. MFIP typically deals with property in the 9th and 17th *arrondissements* where there are the metro links deemed to be important for corporate employees.

At this market level, the accommodation must be well presented and maintained, but the rents achievable reflect this.

Should you require the agent to organise the purchase of an apartment it will add 4 to 5% to the purchase price.

Management contracts (usually running for a year) and agency fees can add up to anywhere between 10% and 50% of the rental income. The upper end of this scale reflects a service which can include all financial arrangements, including marketing and banking, the purchase, crockery, furniture and linen, cleaning, decoration, maintenance, inventories and key holding.

A comparison of like-for-like services suggests that agency fees (and the way they are applied) are surprisingly varied. This seems to depend on:

- The general reputation of the agency. Newcomers appear to under-charge to generate business, but established agencies may prove more reliable.
- The experience and expertise of agencies within certain departments.
- The type of properties the agents are prepared to take on. Some agents are interested only in apartments.

6

Financial Matters

MORTGAGES AND LOANS

When considering mortgage options, a UK borrower usually begins with three basic choices:

- borrowing in the UK against a UK asset or security
- borrowing in France against the security of the property purchased
- remortgaging their UK property.

But you should also :

- Target the amount you require.
- Make sure that your mortgage payments are within your budget.
- Research the market, either personally, or through an independent financial advisor.
- Consider going to your existing lender first. If everything else is equal, this could be the most cost-effective option.
- Decide if you are prepared to forego some short-term flexibility in order to secure a cheaper rate.
- Understand the deals on offer. These include discounted rates, fixed rates, and flexible loans and mortgages linked to other accounts.
- Remember that the headline rate is just one factor. Extras such as legal fees can change the financial equation.
- Do not make more than two formal applications. Your credit reference could be affected.
- Decide your repayment period. Lenders are not always keen

to offer mortgages that run much beyond your retirement date.
● Anticipate that the set-up costs (valuation, legal fees, etc.) will set you back up to €1,100 unless these are bundled into the deal.

It is generally accepted that if you have to borrow it should either be in the currency of your income or in the currency of the country where you are buying the property.

Raising a mortgage or loan in the UK is probably a better option than a French mortgage. This is because UK-based building societies and banks will lend up to 100% (although normally only 95%) of the equity value in your UK property, whereas the French normally set a ceiling of 80%.

In other words if you borrow in the UK against the equity in your own property, the lender is only concerned about the possibility of you defaulting. This keeps things simple.

If the mortgage is only and exclusively on the UK property that you are buying to let, either obtained through an English or French building society or bank, you will be limited to short-term letting. Indeed, a clause in your mortgage contract will prevent you from legally arranging a tenancy of six months or more. This is because it would otherwise be impossible for the financial institution to repossess the property.

The normal lending ceiling is 32% of the total of the client's income per month, which includes any other mortgages. UK mortgages were once almost defined by their 25-year term. The situation is now much more fluid. French mortgages invariably run for 15 years.

The following UK-based financial institutions have recently indicated a willingness to lend money abroad. In each case it is best to begin by approaching your local branch:

● the Abbey National
● the Norwich and Peterborough
● Barclays Bank
● the Newcastle Building Society.

You should also consider approaching an independent UK financial advisor to help you find an appropriate 'buy to let' mortgage. One with a solid track record of honest, independent advice is :

Owen Jackson and Co.,
Linden Place,
Rothbury,
Morpeth,
Northumberland. NE65 7UL
Tel : 01669 621411

Raising finance in the UK

Banks and building societies have competed fiercely for mortgage business in recent years. It should be noted that:

- A mortgage can be secured against assets other than property.
- A bank or building society giving a first mortgage on a UK property will often be willing to extend the facility with the minimum formalities, if the account has been properly conducted.
- UK-based banks and building societies are not generally prepared to lend up to more than 80% of the total equity value of property abroad. This is in line with the policy for French financial institutions.
- Any new mortgage or loan is likely to be subject to legal and arrangement fees.
- Raising money in the UK is generally easier in terms of communication.
- When finance is raised in advance in the UK and deposited in a French bank, you are effectively offering a cash transaction. This can be advantageous in negotiating a reduction in the asking price.

Foreign currency loans

It may be possible to raise foreign currency loans secured against UK property. An advantage of this is that the loan can be fixed for a short repayment period. A loan is charged at a higher interest rate than a mortgage, but because of the repayment period, it is likely to prove to be a less expensive option. A loan may be of particular benefit to people approaching retirement age.

When negotiating loans, banks may ask for insurance cover against default in repayments. This cover is to protect the lending institution, not the borrower, and in the event of a claim this is paid directly to them.

Flexible and saver mortgages

UK financial institutions have introduced several new mortgage schemes during the last few years. Typical amongst the services are those provided by Egg (**www.egg.com**) The advantage of this kind of mortgage is:

- Interest is calculated on a daily, not monthly basis, and your interest will be reduced immediately.
- Over-payments can be made (normally by increasing direct debits or by cheques for £500 or more). These lump sums reduce monthly payments or the length of the mortgage.
- There are rarely early repayment charges. Some of these mortgages also offer a 'draw back facility' which means that, if you make over-payments, you can also make equal withdrawals without any additional charge.
- Transactions can be conducted via the telephone or the internet.
- Statements are normally issued every six months, rather than annually.
- It is sometimes possible to organise a mortgage payment

'holiday', whether or not overpayments have been made.

- These flexible mortgages are normally limited to 85% of the value of the property. Some are also linked to a saver scheme. This is, in effect, a separate account set up to run alongside the mortgage account. When the amount of interest on the mortgage is calculated, the customer is only charged on the difference between the amount he owes on the mortgage account and the amount of savings in the savings account. This is now popularly known as 'off-setting'. Interest is not usually paid on the savings balance and, if this balance becomes greater than the mortgage balance, the lending institution will ask you to transfer the difference to an interest-bearing savings account. These savings-linked mortgages may attract the attention of the Chancellor of the Exchequer because, as no interest is paid on the savings account, it is not taxable.

- The financial institutions offering these flexible mortgages are normally associated with insurance companies who can offer competitive quotes on insurance for life and critical illness, mortgage payment protection, buildings and contents.

Bank account mortgages

These are offered by a number of financial institutions. The idea is basically to combine the features of a current account with a ranged overdraft fixed to the equity value of a property.

As with the flexible mortgage above, there are advantages in terms of paying off the loan more quickly and an ability to borrow at any time up to the agreed limit. The major critical disadvantage is the time period which, though flexible, is conditioned by circumstances such as your proposed retirement date. But the definition of retirement is not always straightforward. Are you, for instance, 'retired' when you leave your regular employment or business in the UK to set up a *gîte* enterprise in France?

An endowment mortgage

Borrowers may be offered loans which include linkage to endowment and/or pension plans. Packages of this kind are often more for the benefit of the lender than the borrower, who most frequently would be better off with a simple repayment scheme. In recent years, some forms of endowment have not paid off, and borrowers should be very cautious about entering into this kind of arrangement.

Raising finance in France

Many financial institutions in France offer loans, but it is principally the banks that provide mortgage finance. A French loan is certainly a different option:

- Interest rates in France have been historically lower than those in the UK, although the differential is now small. Attractive government subsidies can apply to the purchase of a main residence, but these loans are difficult, sometimes impossible, to obtain. However, if you accept a subsidy loan, you undertake to live in the premises for a minimum of eight months a year. This, in turn, has tax implications because you then become legally domiciled in France.
- Interest rates are fixed for the whole term of the mortgage. This, of course, is only advantageous if bank rate rises.
- Reversible rate mortgages are negotiable. This means that the interest rate is fixed for a period and then revised within certain parameters. When interest rates are high, or it is anticipated that they will become so, this can be the best option.
- French financial institutions charge around 1% of the total loan as an arrangement fee.
- Some borrowers may be eligible for a special savings loan. This is set at below normal rates which do not require the purchaser to become domiciled in France. Loans can be

negotiated in a number of different currencies. This is partly speculative and partly created by market perception that some currencies are more stable than others.

● Security on the property will be required, and loans are never more than 80% of the purchase price. Premiums for life, health and disability insurance are invariably included in the package.

● You will not be sold endowments or pension mortgage packages by French banks. They simply do not exist.

● The law requires a 'cooling off' period (a minimum of 10 days) after a formal mortgage offer.

When checking current repayment rates of UK and French mortgages, it is important to compare like with like. Take into account the term of years offered (normally shorter in France) and add insurance arrangements and legal fees. UK financial institutions are sometimes coy about revealing the rates of commission they charge.

The following major French institutions are enthusiastic enough about UK mortgage business to have opened offices on this side of the Channel. They also provide brochures and free information:

The Banque Transatlantique
36 St James's Street
London
SW1A1JD
Tel : 020 7493 6717

Credit Agricole
11 Moorfields Highwalk
London
EC2Y9DE
Tel : 020 7374 5000

Credit Lyonnais
Suite 57
1 Colme Street
Edinburgh
EH36AA
Tel : 0131 220 8257

Credit du Nord
6th Floor
Exchange House
Primrose Street
London
EC2 2ED
Tel : 020 7488 0872

In addition to the major banking organisations, loans can be negotiated through French savings banks and *notaires*. All loans are subject to your financial status but, again, the general rule is that your mortgage repayments and normal outgoings should not add up to more than 32% of your gross income.

BANKING IN FRANCE

Even if you do not intend to live in France it is well worth considering a French bank account – at least until the UK embraces the euro. If nothing else, this will save the cost of currency exchanges.

Although it is theoretically possible for property owners in France to manage without a French bank account, it is more convenient to have one. French banking rules are, however, rather different to those in most EU countries. It is best to be aware of the way the system works.

Opening a French bank account

Foreigners can open a special account called a *'compte étranger'* (literally a stranger's account). The French government has sought to reduce tax evasion by discouraging 'cash' deals. This means that notes and coinage cannot be paid into bank accounts. The *compte étranger* can be an ordinary/current account (*compte chéques*) or a deposit account (*compte sur livret*). The ordinary account provides you with a chequebook, and the deposit account pays interest, although in the present financial climate the return is almost so low as to be discounted. Orders for new chequebooks can take several weeks to process so it is best to keep a spare book.

Arrangements for statements are similar to those enforced in the UK, but it is unwise to assume that your statement is up to date. There are good reasons why the French clearing system is referred to as *la tortue* – the tortoise.

When you open an account, the bank will check with central records to find out if you are subject to an interdiction – banned from holding a bank account. Inter-bank communication is good. A UK bankruptcy, a withdrawal of credit notice, or a court order for debt or non-payment, will almost certainly prevent you from opening an ordinary account.

There is also a potential Catch 22 here. It can be difficult to open a French account without an address in France. It can be equally difficult to follow through the purchase process without a French account. But French banks understand money. Explain your intentions and circumstances carefully. There is always another bank across the street.

Interest

Gross interest is paid on deposit accounts. It is your responsibility to declare this to the taxman either in France or in the UK. The double taxation agreement between the countries means you are only liable to pay tax once; normally you would choose to pay that tax in the UK. This is partly because of the generally more beneficial tax regime and because certain elements of income – such as some pensions – will automatically be subject to the UK tax regime. Most banks impose a minimum balance requirement for ordinary accounts – usually around €100.

Credits and debits

Cheques paid into your account are credited on the same day, even if post-dated, but you cannot draw against them until clearance is complete.
French cheques are similar to their UK counterparts, with the amount written in both words and numbers. If the amounts are different, the words will be assumed to be correct. Cheques must be endorsed. Open cheques will be honoured but this can lead to delay. Crossed cheques are recommended. Cheques can only be stopped for security reasons – this generally means notifying the bank that a cheque has been lost or stolen.

Using – and misusing – your cheques

Cheque guarantee cards are not issued in France, but some form of proof of identity is likely to be required for all transactions. French nationals carry identity cards.

The French are very tough on the misuse of bank accounts. If you bounce a cheque, the bank will instruct you to put matters right. If you fail to do so within a 30-day limit, your chequebook will be withdrawn, your account frozen and you will be subject to a ban (an interdiction). The ban is recorded with the Banque de France and the file is retained for two years, during which time you may not open a bank account in France. Even if your account is regularised within the required 30 days, a second offence within a year will incur a 12-month chequebook ban.

Financial penalties for bouncing cheques are also severe. These can range from a fine of €450 – €40,000. Prison sentences of up to five years can be (and occasionally are) imposed. Misunderstanding the system, or claiming that the problem arose through the slowness of the clearing system, have not proved to be adequate defences in law.

UK BANKS IN FRANCE

All major UK banks are represented in France although, outside the major cities, the branches are thinly distributed. The advantage of dealing with a UK bank in France is primarily one of communication. Banks of all nationalities are subject to French banking law.

CREDIT CARDS

The use of plastic is now commonplace in France. All French credit cards are now *'cartes des puces'* (quite literally, 'flea cards') because they have a microchip embedded in them. After paying at a cash desk, owners simply enter their pin number into a hand-held input machine to confirm the transaction. This system is now being introduced in the UK. Unfortunately the technology is different and, on this occasion, it is the French who are out of step with Europe. So hang on to your UK card. All will be well – eventually.

The Visa group is by far the most useful, as Visa is automatically part of the *Carte Bancaire* group, but a larger number of points of sale are now accepting Mastercard. UK PINS are accepted by most dispensers for cash withdrawals. Statements can be sent directly from the UK.

INSURANCE

Insurance premiums in France are different in character from those in the UK:

- The law demands that every property is covered by third party insurance (*civile propriété*). If your property is to be built, a premium must be paid before work on the site commences.
- French mortgage lenders, unlike their UK equivalents, do not insist that you take out buildings insurance. However, it is

strongly recommended that you do so. This can be arranged separately or included in a comprehensive policy (*multirisque*) that also covers your possessions.

● UK insurers generally offer the most complete and competitive policies but be aware that policies linked to household and buildings insurance often include 'residential' clauses. This frequently means that, if you are away from the property for more than 30 consecutive days, the cover is invalid.

● If you live in a block of flats the *civile propriété* and buildings policies will be paid communally. Check your lease for the terms.

● If you are living in France you should seriously consider 'top up' health insurance for yourself and your family. The French Health Service is wonderful but massively in debt. It is thought to be inevitable that the E111 will come to cover basic and emergency treatment.

Who is responsible?

If you let out your property, or allow someone to live in it, the tenant should indemnify you against certain risks. This, most importantly, includes the risks against fire and inundation.

The tenant is responsible for insuring his own possessions but there are some grey areas. As a rule of thumb, assume that if something is fixed (such as a kitchen unit) or permanently placed (such as a large bookcase) it will be generally considered that this is the owner's responsibility. Personal clothing, hi-fi equipment, cameras, and jewellery will generally be assumed to be the tenant's.

The guidelines are :

● Is the item concerned listed on the inventory? If so it will be the owner's responsibility.

● Is the item small enough to be regularly transported outside the premises? If so it will be the tenant's responsibility.

But again there are grey areas. Recent rulings suggest that televisions are 'portable' (and therefore transportable) if they have a carrying handle. Responsibility for a vacuum cleaner recently occupied French legal minds for several months. The outcome was that a vacuum cleaner should be the owner's responsibility where the tenancies were short-term and the tenant's responsibility when leases were for six months or longer.

The precise insurance requirements of buying to let depend on the way the business is set up. If the business is, for instance, a limited company, it becomes a separate legal entity and will require its own insurance. Otherwise, the rules apply exactly as they would to an individual trader. The insurers also need to know when the property is 'a business' because of the rules on public indemnity insurance. You will also require the normal insurance against loss and on the property and its contents.

Thought should also be given to the motor insurance requirements. If your visits to France are primarily in connection with the property and the letting business it would be difficult to argue, in the event of a claim, that normal social, domestic and pleasure insurance was adequate cover.

Business cover

All registered businesses are expected to have the following insurance cover:

- motor insurance for vehicles owned by the company
- a health insurance 'top up' policy for employees
- business property insurance against fire, theft, storm and water damage, and the breakage of glass.

Additional cover

Standard business cover is regarded as a legal minimum. Many companies also pay premiums for:

- pensions and saving schemes
- accident and death at work
- consequential loss following fire, flood, or other 'natural' events
- legal liability as to the owner or tenant of the building
- cafés, hotels, restaurants, garages, and *gîtes*, require public liability cover.

Job related cover

Certain types of enterprise require additional insurance cover. Architects, lawyers, and doctors require professional indemnity insurance.

Renewals

French policies are automatically renewed unless written notice is given two months before the renewal date.

Claims

All claims must be notified within five working days. This is reduced to 24 hours in the case of theft.

Premium costs

These have been traditionally comparable with the UK. Also comparable is the way that premiums in certain areas, and for certain risks, have rocketed in recent years. The insurance companies tell us that this is primarily because of increasing crime and fraudulent claims. There is little doubt, however, that this also has much to do with a downturn in insurance companies' overall profitability because of the downturn of the worldwide stock market.

All French insurance policies follow a format prescribed by law:

- The risks and exclusions must be fully described.
- The level of cover and the obligations of both insurer and insured must be identified.

The schedule describes matters that relate to the issue of the policy. These include registered addresses, the premium paid and renewable dates.

Premium taxes

Insurance premiums are subject to tax at the following rates:

- motor vehicles   34.9%
- fire and combined policies   7% to 30%
- health policies   9%

The documentation format

All French insurance policies follow a format prescribed by law:

- The risks and exclusions must be fully described.
- The level of cover and the obligations of both insurer and insured must be identified.
- The schedule describes matters that relate to the issue of the policy. These include registered addresses, the premium paid, and the renewal dates.

7

Taxation

Although many UK owners of French property opt to pay income tax in the UK, this does not mean that they can avoid French taxation altogether. Principally these taxes are:

- land tax (*taxe fonciere*)
- community tax (*taxe d'habitation*)
- capital gains tax (*régime des plus-values des particuliers*).

And, under certain circumstances, you may also be liable for:

- inheritance tax (*droits de succession*)
- gift tax (*droits de donation*).

REGISTRATION

The ownership of all French property must be registered with the French tax authorities. Owners who are not residents have to register by 30 April following completion of the property purchase. Residents are expected to register immediately with the local tax office (*Centre des Impôts*). Non-resident owners should register with the tax centre for non-residents at:

Centre des Impôts des Non-residents
9 Rue d'Uzes
75094 Paris

DOMICILE

For tax purposes the concept of domicile is important in Europe, as certain domiciles have been seen as offering very favourable tax regimes. These include the Isle of Man, Jersey, Liechtenstein and Monaco. However, to be domiciled in these countries (unless you are native) is exclusive to the very rich. The general rule is that you will pay income tax in the country in which you are deemed to be domiciled. Those domiciled outside France will only pay tax on the portion of their personal income earned within the country. You will be said to have a French *fiscal domicile* if:

- You have a home in France and you spend more than 183 days in the country within any financial year.
- Your wife and family live in France for more than 183 days in any financial year.
- You work in France on either a salaried or self-employed basis, unless you can prove that your work is ancillary to your main employment. This can be a problem for those buying to let in France, particularly for those who no longer have any regular employment elsewhere. Fortunately, 'employment' can be deemed to include receiving a pension in the UK and/or other benefits or allowances.
- Most of your income is generated in France. This could for instance catch retired people who run a *gîte* business which generates a greater income than their UK pensions.

The concept of domicile is critical. The French authorities, naturally, wish to burden you with as much tax as possible. This is best avoided in anticipation by being clear about your own position and discussing it with the French tax authorities before submitting your first return.

INCOME TAX

If you are domiciled in France you may be liable to pay income tax. There are some anomalies here. An occupational pension – such as that received by teachers and civil servants – will attract income tax in the UK; a personal pension, however, will attract personal income tax if you are domiciled in France.

French tax laws are complex and there will, inevitably, be winners and losers when compared with the UK tax regime. Long-term residents sometimes choose to take French citizenship because foreigners are subject to an increasingly heavy burden of personal taxation. It is also possible, even prudent, to take the view that, if you are to benefit from the French health and welfare systems, it is better to be working towards French citizenship.

There is an outline of the system below. Detailed information is available from a French government interdepartmental economic agency – *Le Délégation à l'Aménagement du Territoire et à l'Action Régionale* (DATAR). Their UK address is:

21–24 Grosvenor Place
London
SW1X 7HU
Tel : 020 7823 1895

Essentially, DATAR's UK office is intended to offer fiscal advice to anyone considering selling in the French market-place or setting up a business in France. A letting business comes within this framework. DATAR's publications can be obtained from:

1 Avenue Charles Floquet
75007 Paris
Tel : 00331 47 83 61 20
Fax : 00331 40 65 12 34

French income tax is assessed on a family basis. The husband is responsible for the annual return which includes the income of his wife, and children who are still in the education system, or doing national service. Divorced, separated or widowed persons claim allowances according to personal circumstances. Across the board allowances include:

- money spent on major property repairs
- money spent on 'green' projects such as the installation of solar panels for heating, cavity wall insulation, and double-glazing
- payments for maintenance of dependent relatives other than children
- gifts to charity
- contributions to the *sécurité sociale*
- approved life-insurance premiums
- interest payments on certain loans
- special arrangements for single parents with young children.

Taxable income is worked out by deducting allowances from total income and dividing the net figure by:

- a factor of one for a single person with no children
- two for a married couple with no children
- two and a half for a married couple with one child
- an extra half for each additional child (under the age of 18 or in full time education). A married couple with four children will, thus, divide by four.

When taxable income has been assessed, the rates that apply fall into a band system. The following are approximate figures for those incurring income tax liability in France in 2002. These bands, however, are subject to change and should be treated only as a rough guide:

The first € 5,666 of taxable income is tax-free.

€ 5,666 to € 6,166	–	5%
€ 6,166 to € 7,000	–	10%
€ 7,001 to € 10,833	–	15%
€ 10,834 to € 14,000	–	20%
€ 14,001 to € 18,333	–	25%
€ 18,334 to € 21,333	–	30%
€ 21,334 to € 25,333	–	35%
€ 25,334 to € 41,000	–	40%
€ 41,001 to € 58,000	–	45%
€ 58,001 to € 67,166	–	50%
€ 67,167 to € 77,333	–	55%
€ 77,334 upwards	–	58%

A married couple with no children, no allowances and a joint income of €41,666 would pay tax as follows (half of €41,666 is €20,833, so each has a taxable income of €20,833):

On the first € 5,666	– no tax is paid	
On the next € 500 at 5%	–	€ 25
On the next € 833 at 10%	–	€ 83
On the next € 3,833 at 15%	–	€ 575
On the next € 3,166 at 20%	–	€ 633
On the next € 4,333 at 25%	–	€1,083
On the next € 2,500 at 30%	–	€ 833
Total		€3,233

Their joint tax bill would be (€ 3233 x 2) €6,466

The same couple living in England would automatically have personal allowances of € 7,555 each. Their joint tax bill would therefore look like this:

First taxable income € 20,833 – € 7,555	=	€ 13,278
Tax on €13,278 at 20%	=	€ 2,656
Tax on € 10,600 at 4%	=	€ 424
Less allowance to reduce tax on €2900 at 15% =		€ 435

Therefore, tax paid is €2,645

As the spouse is treated exactly the same, their joint tax bill
would be :

$$(€2,645x2) \quad = \quad €5,290$$

The French tax system benefits large families and people on low
incomes. The tax year runs from 1 January, and bills are paid in
three equal instalments in the year following the liability.
Filling in a tax return is difficult because of the technical
language involved. English-speaking residents paying income
tax in France invariably require the services of an accountant.
When the authorities suspect that tax declarations are
inaccurate or fraudulent, they investigate. In certain
circumstances, residents with complex tax affairs (including
perhaps income from a number of sources outside France) will
be assessed according to the punitive *régime de l'imposition
forfaiture*. Under this system, income is assessed according to
arbitrary norms. This includes ascribing letting value to all
properties you own and multiplying it by a factor of three or
five. Cars are valued and taxed at 75% of their maximum new
showroom value, employees are assumed to have massive
salaries, and racehorses are reckoned as winners.

LAND TAX

Taxe foncière is levied by the local *commune* and is similar to
the system of parish rates in the UK. Registers of all property
and owners are maintained at the *mairie*.
   Property is given a notional letting value on which the *taxe
foncière* is based. Exceptions include government and public
buildings, winepresses and stables. New buildings are exempt
from tax for two years.
   The last general valuation of buildings was carried out in 1974.
The tax levied is adjusted annually in line with the inflation index.
It is an inevitable truth that rural properties are less heavily taxed.

COMMUNITY TAX

Taxe d'habitation is paid by the resident occupier of a property on 1 January each year. It is calculated according to the value of amenities. These include the size of the property, including garages, outbuildings and land. If the property is not subject to a lease then the owner of the property is liable for the payment of tax.

This tax is reduced when the property is used as the principal residence of a family. If, therefore, you have purchased a large property to let but live in a portion of it, the tax will be reduced. Since 1989, each *commune* has a fixed *taxe d'habitation* at rates of 5, 10 or 15% of the notional letting value.

Both *taxe foncière* and *taxe d'habitation* are payable by UK residents, whether or not the property is designated as their main residence. Again rural properties suffer a lower burden of tax.

CAPITAL GAINS TAX

The *régime des plus-values des particuliers* is imposed on anyone who is domiciled in France when assets are sold. It is important to note, however, that their primary residence is exempt. It is generally applied to residents (domiciled elsewhere) who sell any property in France.

The tax is levied at 33%. The capital gain is deemed to be the difference between the purchase price and the sale price, but the seller can offset:

- the supplementary costs of making the purchase, or 10% of the purchase price, whichever is the higher figure;
- an indexation of the increase in property values according to government figures.

This tax is intended to catch primarily those profiting from property dealing. French law demands that foreign sellers employ an agent to handle the sale of property. This agent (normally a *notaire*) is responsible for paying the tax to the government.

In practice, the capital gains tax payable on the property sale is likely to be modest or non-existent. But those who improve property considerably, or create integral residential units (such as a granny flat), could find themselves paying for the privilege. For company-held property the tax is divided into short-and long-term gains. Short-term is defined by assets held. It also includes a portion of the revaluation of depreciable fixed assets held for less than two years. Long-term gains are the sale of assets held for more than two years. The rates are:

● short-term gains – 39%
● long-term gains – 25% for land assets and 19% for fixed assets. If a company is subject to corporation tax, this last figure is reduced to 16%.

VALUE ADDED TAX

The sale of new properties (or any sale within five years of construction) is subject to VAT (*TVA*). This should be included in the sale price and paid by the developer.

Property resold within that five-year period is also subject to *TVA*. This concerns UK buyers more than is necessary. The amount is not usually considerable because the seller offsets the amount paid in *TVA* on the initial sale. Only when a property has been substantially improved within the five-year period is it likely to attract a significant *TVA* bill.

All business operations in France are theoretically liable for *TVA* as long as an 'economic activity' is involved. This would apply, for instance, to a *gîte* business. This is different to the UK situation, where many small businesses fall below the threshold.

'Economic activity' is conditioned by the nature of that activity and the business itself. In general, the rules are:

- Those involved in agricultural, trading, manufacturing, and service industries are required to register.
- Salaried activities are normally exempt, as are insurance and medical activities, educational services, and transactions subject to other taxes. Those in the 'buy to let' sector have sometimes taken advantage of the educational services' 'exemption' by gilding holiday packages with educational activities. The *TVA* man invariably looks closely at packages of this kind. Success in applying for this exemption will depend on the educational content involved. If this is seen to be peripheral, i.e. if there are no experienced qualified instructors, defined course content, and some sort of 'qualification', the exemption is unlikely to be accepted.
- Special rules apply to advertising, staffing agencies, research, and the hire of equipment and machinery.

TVA is assessed on the value added for each stage of production. A credit system is applied through which *TVA* is charged down the chain of production to the point of sale. At this stage, the bill is finally paid by the customer.

The assessment applies to all amounts received by sellers and suppliers in exchange for the services received or the goods sold. In the case of a product, tax liability is incurred at the time the goods are delivered. Services can be paid on an accruals basis. The *TVA* payable is calculated by deducting input from output *TVA*. Any excess will be refunded.

Form CA3

The standard *TVA* form (CA3), must be completed quarterly by small businesses. These are defined as companies that do not pay capital gains tax. Other businesses must make out a monthly return.

CAR TAX

Although tax on privately-owned vehicles was abolished in 2002, tax on company-owned vehicles was not. The amount payable depends on the horsepower of the vehicle. The rate varies between €1,000 and €2,000.

Île de France

An additional annual levy is charged on prime commercial sites in the Île de France region. This varies between €3 and €10 per square metre of the surface area.

INITIAL TAX LIABILITY

Initial tax liability depends on whether you are starting a new business or taking over an existing one.

Starting a new business normally involves the purchase of a *fonds de commerce*. Taking over a new business involves paying transfer duties (*droits d'enregistrement*). The transfer duties apply to all assets transferred, apart from goods subject to *TVA*.

Transfer duty (*droits d'enregistrement*)

If you are taking over an existing letting business this may be subject to transfer duty. The existing scale of charges is:

Table 7.1 Transfer duty charges

Property value	National	Department	Local	Total
Less than € 15,250	Nil	Nil	Nil	Nil
From € 15,251 to €45,750	6%	0.6%	0.4%	7%
In excess of € 45,751	11.8%	1.4%	1%	14.2%

In the case of a business take-over there is a one-off transfer duty charge of 4.8%. If however the new company is formed as a *société anonyme* (a type of limited company) there is no duty payable – as long as the transfer took place outside France. Capital gains tax is not applied to business purchases.

Business licence tax (*taxe professionnelle*)

The tax is primarily targeted at the proprietors of offices and shops. Owners of *gîtes*, bed and breakfast accommodation, and long-term rental property are generally exempt.

In many ways, the tax is similar to the business rates system formerly applied in the UK. It is based on an agreed rental value of fixed assets. This includes a notional market value of a rented property. A distinctly French feature of the tax is that the fixed assets figure is taken to include 18% of salaries paid in the tax year before last.

The taxes are abated in the first year, then generally on a sliding scale for five years.

The amount levied can vary enormously in percentage terms according to local incentives to attract business. To complicate matters further *taxe professionnelle* is a political hot potato. The policy, and therefore the amount charged, can change considerably following each round of local government elections.

In the year 2004, the lowest rate of *taxe professionnelle* levied in France was 10%, the highest was 26% and the median national average was 17.14%.

A typical small business bill may look like this:

- Value of property   €100,000
- Value of additional fixed assets   € 25,000
- 18% of payroll   € 12,500
- Total charge value   €137,500
- The total tax payable at national median
      rate (17.14%)   € 23,567

CORPORATION TAX (*IMPÔTS SUR LES SOCIÉTÉS*)

All businesses registered in France are subject to corporation tax apart from:

- new businesses, which are exempt for three years
- certain small businesses eligible for taxation under the simplified business income scheme. This exemption would normally apply to *gîte* owners.

The tax is currently 42% of distributed profits, and 39% of undistributed profits. It is collected quarterly. A definition of taxable profit is similar to the formula applied in the UK. The main elements are:

- The difference between the cost value of stock at the beginning and the end of the year. Added to this is the value of the services, subsidies, and income from fringe profits such as interest payments.
- Allowable expenses to set against this include: salaries, welfare payments, interest and loans, depreciation of equipment, education and training expenses, and the purchase of certain goods necessary for the running of the business.

TAXATION OF BUSINESS INCOME (*IMPÔTS SUR LES BÉNÉFICES INDUSTRIELLES ET COMMERCIAUX*)

This is the small business alternative to corporation tax. The definition of a small business can be complex, but is normally taken to include:

- sole traders
- a partnership based on a limited liability company
- a family-owned limited liability company.

Businesses that qualify have profits taxed on a basis very similar to that of personal income tax, although taxable profits are calculated as for corporation tax. Business income scheme taxation has advantages when the chargeable rate of income tax is lower than the corporation tax. This applies to most small businesses. In exceptional circumstances, however, it may be advantageous to change the legal identity of the business in order to fall into the net of corporation tax.

WILLS AND INHERITANCE

When you own French property, the rules concerning its disposition are French. Even if a dispute about ownership or inheritance originates in the UK, the law that will decide the outcome will be French.

French law is very concerned with the idea of passing down assets within a family. This is the guiding principle of rights of succession. There have been some recent changes, largely concerned with protecting the interests of a surviving partner.

Rules of Succession

French succession laws were drafted at the time of Napoleon, partly to prevent what had previously been seen as the 'scandal of the rich'. This 'scandal' included the dispersal of property to mistresses (otherwise described as 'housekeepers', 'wards', and 'nieces' and their offspring), to the exclusion of 'natural' heirs. It is said that the last three kings of France, before the revolution of 1789, generously disposed of some 30 châteaux and country estates, some 10% of the crown revenue, and an almost incalculable number of honours and commissions to their mistresses and illegitimate children. The somewhat draconian rules of succession in force today are said to result, in part, from Napoleon's abhorrence of the abuse of power and revenues in this way. Napoleon himself only gave away land (and kingdoms) that he had conquered beyond the boundaries of France.

The French are, therefore, required by law to leave most of their estate to their family. French residents' assets are dealt with under the rules of domicile, but these do not include, property which is always passed on according to laws of succession. Precedence is given to the ascendant and descendant heirs. Briefly, the inheritance rules are:

- One child will inherit at least half the estate.
- Two children between them will inherit at least two-thirds of the estate.
- Three or more children will share at least three-quarters of the estate.
- The surviving spouse will inherit half, one third or a quarter of the estate, or a life interest in the estate which will pass to the children on his or her demise.
- The remaining portion of the estate is freely disposable. If there are no surviving ascendants, descendants, or spouse, the entire estate would becomes freely disposable.
- The surviving spouse is entitled to continue to enjoy the marital property during his or her lifetime.

French residents have tried various ploys to get round the rules of succession. One is to create a trust, but trusts appearing to alters the rights of succession have generally not been recognised in French courts.

There used to be only one legal way to offset some of the impact of the inheritance rules. This was to arrange the property purchase as a co-ownership with a contract clause that allows the surviving partner to inherit. The survivor could then choose:

- to sell the property and take the proceeds beyond the rule of French law. It is worth noting that although currency control laws have long gone it is still illegal to export, without consent, more than €50,000 in cash.
- to stay in the property as sole owner. If this happens, the estate of the survivor will become subject to the normal rules of domicile and succession.

A *notaire* can draw up a contract of co-ownership, though he would be surprised if he was asked to perform this service for a married couple.

The new law (effective from the summer of 2003) is likely to simplify matters considerably although it will only apply if the property is held in joint names. In these circumstances the whole property can pass automatically to the surviving spouse although the rest of the estate will still be disposed of according to the rules of succession.

Alternatively, married couples can arrange for an '*en tontine*' clause to be incorporated within the deeds at the time of purchase. *En tontine* was originally intended to avoid the break-up of large estates. Traditionally, it meant that those who would ordinarily have rights under the rules of succession are bypassed in favour of the family member who survived longest. Typically, half a dozen brothers working a farm would agree that the property should pass undivided to the last of them still living and working the farm. A similar arrangement was outlawed in the UK more than a century ago because it led, quite literally, to murder.

En tontine in France is now invariably restricted to married couples. When the first partner dies, the survivor becomes the absolute owner of the property. Typically the form is:

'*. . . that it is expressly agreed between the purchasers that the first to die will be deemed never to have had any right to the property . . . and the said property will be deemed to have always been that of the survivor.*

'*Until the death of the first purchaser each purchaser shall be joint owner. Neither of them can sell the property, and any act of management or of disposal must take place with the unanimous consent of both purchasers. The purchasers declare that they have taken into account the chancy nature of this arrangement in determining the share of the purchase price payable by each of them.*'

An *en tontine* clause is sometimes appropriate for married

couples if neither partner has children by previous marriages. This is because *en tontine* can be challenged by children on the grounds that the clause deprives them of their rights under the French succession rules. And, under the *en tontine* clause, the surviving spouse has to pay French succession tax at the rate of 60% of one half of the value of the property.

Neither co-ownership or an *en tontine* clause can avoid succession duties. They do, however, generally delay their imposition and may also help to ensure that the property is disposed of according to the owners' wishes.

Inheritance Rules and Tax

● Payments are made by those who inherit according to the value of the assets they receive and their relationship to the deceased.
● All assets in France are subject to rights of succession.
● The assets of those domiciled in France include property, at home and abroad.
● The assets of those not domiciled in France exclude property outside French borders.

The rates of inheritance tax given below are based on current bands:

● When an estate passes to the surviving spouse or a relative in direct ascendant or descendant line, there is a tax-free allowance of €45,000 per beneficiary.
● After that, the surviving spouse pays:

5% on the next € 8,333
10% on amounts between €8,333 and €16,666
15% on amounts between €16,666 and €33,333
20% on amounts between €33,333 and €566,666
30% on amounts between €566,666 and €933,333
35% on amounts between €933,333 and €2,000,000
40% on amounts in excess of € 2,000,000

● The ascendant or descendant relative pays:

5% on the next € 8,333
10% on amounts between € 8,333 and € 12,500
15% on amounts between € 12,500 and € 15,666
20% on amounts between € 15,666 and € 566,666
25% on amounts between € 566,666 and € 933,333
30% on amounts between € 933,333 and € 2,000,000
40% on amounts in excess of € 2,000,000

● Divorced or unmarried brothers and sisters have a beneficiary allowance of € 16,666. The same allowance can be claimed if they are more than 50 years of age or suffer from infirmity. After this they pay:

35% on all amounts up to €25,000
45% on amounts above €25,000

● Third degree relatives – aunts, uncles, nephews, nieces and cousins – pay 55% of the inheritance received.
● Any other beneficiary (apart from certain charities) will pay a rate of 60%.

Gift Tax

The rules for *droits de donation* are similar to those applied above. The idea is to prevent the avoidance of inheritance tax. There is some mitigation for:

● gifts given as wedding presents
● gifts made by people under the age of 65.

Livret de famille

French families are required to keep a *livret de famille* (family booklet). A marriage opens a new *livret* and details of birth, adoptions, and deaths are added. If a couple divorce, two separate copies are created and when a death occurs, the *livret* is handed in.

It is an offence not to keep the *livret* up to date. Although the French issue certificates for births, marriages and deaths, it is the *livret* that provides the owner's proof in the law of inheritance.
Non-French residents are not required to maintain a *livret*. However, the *livret* demonstrates two things:

● The French are keen on written evidence. Proving a will in France may be difficult without a full set of family certificates, affidavits, and decrees.
● There are important precedents in French civil law about the status of the family and the members of the family group. This begins to explain why rules of succession are more important than the wishes of individuals in the matter of inheritance. Under French law it is impossible to give away the bulk of an estate to a cats' home whilst depriving your children of their inheritance.

The will as a document

Three kinds of will are provable under French law:

● The *testament olographe* is hand-written, signed and dated by the testator. Any additions, including the signature of a witness, will invalidate it.
● The *testament authentique* is dictated by the testator and witnessed by two *notaires*, or one *notaire* and two other adult witnesses.
● The *testament mystique* is a handwritten or typescript document signed by the testator and sealed in an envelope in the presence of two witnesses. The witnesses then hand the envelope to a *notaire* who signs the sealed envelope himself. He dates it, notes the names of the witnesses, and adds a written declaration that he understands the envelope to contain the will of a named testator.

Rules for validating wills in France are strict. The more complex the document, the more likely it is to become void.

Rules on intestacy in France are also different. In France, the whole of the property would be divided according to the laws of succession, which favour children rather than the surviving spouse. It is also worth noting that in France, marriages do not automatically invalidate an existing will.

Intestacy profits nobody but lawyers, and this is doubly true for double intestacy. The importance of taking good advice when property and assets are held in more than one country cannot be overstated.

Executors

In the UK, an executor is technically the owner of the testator's assets and property. He discharges the responsibility of ownership by paying debts and duties and then distributing the residue of the estate in accordance with the testator's wishes.

In France, the position is different. Property is deemed to pass directly to heirs under the rules of succession and an executor is not necessary. Debts and duties are the responsibility of the heirs, but an *executeur testamentaire* may be appointed to help supervise other aspects of the process of inheritance.

This service is important if specific items of furniture and jewellery are intended to pass to the named beneficiaries within that part of the estate which is freely disposable. Any adult who accepts the responsibility must be named in the will and should not be a major beneficiary.

MARRIAGE CONTRACTS

The French have a choice as to how assets are held by married couples. This choice is recorded as a contract which is drawn up by the *notaire* before the wedding. If no such contract is agreed, the law assumes the married couple are subject to the *régime de communauté reduité aux acque^ts*. Briefly, this means that assets belonging to each of the married couple at the time of the wedding remain their personal property, but later assets they acquire together are to be equally divided in the event of a divorce. This is the most common form of written or implied contract. There are, however, three alternatives:

- *Régime de la séparation des biens.* This is similar to the legal position in the UK. In effect, husband and wife each retain their own assets.
- *Régime de la participation aux acqueˆts.* Here the husband places limitations on the sharing of assets.
- *Régime de cummunauté universelle.* Here, all assets are shared regardless of who brought them into the marriage.

8

A Head for Business

PREPARING FOR PROFIT

Perhaps the worst mistake you can make in the 'buy to rent' business is to over-estimate profitability.

A dream turns to nightmare

Imagine buying a €500,000 house in Southern Brittany and anticipating the not unreasonable future rental income of say €2,500 per week in the summer months. Set alongside this the idea that the house will run itself in terms of costs, and profits can be put towards the mortgage. All this may seem realistic, even achievable.

But what if things do not pan out as they should? To begin with, your tenants may not be reasonable. Some people will complain in the hope of achieving a rebate or even freeloading. Visitors from the United States in particular, have been known to demand air-conditioning units in every room, safety barriers around a paddling pool, garbage disposal units and fridges the size of billiard tables. Professional agents normally deal with these kinds of complaints better than owners.

But is all too easy to blame the tenants for things that go wrong. French lawyers, who are a mine of information on holiday rental problems, often believe it is the desire of the owner to save money that leads to most of the difficulties. It is also suggested that many UK buyers 'leave their brains behind on the aeroplane'.

Ask yourself the following questions:

- Will you be able to go to France and manage everything yourself?
- How would you respond, as a visitor, if you believed that too many corners had been cut?
- What strategies can you put in place for vetting potential holiday tenants? Renters have often found out to their cost that 'Hooray Henry types' are most likely to abuse your property. The advice here, if you are not using a professional letting agent, is to establish and maintain personal contact with your visitors. A booking made via the internet can be dangerously impersonal.

Assess your outgoings and expenses objectively. Bear in mind that this can include wealth tax, land tax and habitation tax. There is also water, insurance, electricity and gas. And don't forget to be realistic about the cost of the general maintenance. And, that € million residence on the Côte d'Azur could be subject to the scorching sun and flooding. Sometimes, there may not be enough water. Concrete structures crack quite readily and swimming pool maintenance and cleaning costs can be horrendous.

Also remember that cleaning staff in the South of France will charge a minimum of €12 an hour and it can be tricky to find someone reliable. If you are not looking after the property personally, what arrangements are put in place for a leak or mechanical failure? A house manager is one answer, but this would cost you € 600 per month.

And even the better-behaved guests are unlikely to behave in the same decorous manner as they would at home. There are stories of cream carpets covered in chocolate, and huge telephone bills. But will you really throw the phone out and ask your prospective holiday tenant for a massive deposit? And, in a luxury villa, even a €10,000 deposit may not cover the damage created by a particularly exuberant family.

Paying your dues

There is strong anecdotal evidence that many UK owners do not declare their rental income. Whilst the temptation to 'cheat' is strong, it may be as unnecessary as it can be dangerous. In the first place, the margin of profit, particularly in the first year, is likely to be modest and the tax breaks worthwhile. Remember also that legitimate expenses and set-up costs can be set against income.

It is sometimes argued that the best way to avoid tax is to let property only to people you know. The assumption is that people you know are less likely 'to drop you in it' than those you do not. The evidence of human nature, however, suggests that the opposite is more likely to be the case.

The cheapest option

Perhaps the cheapest option for marketing a holiday let is to go to a website such as **www.frenchconnections.co.uk** or **www.frenchcountry.co.uk** You will pay an annual fee of between €120 and €170 for an advertisement with pictures. Potential clients will theoretically contact the owner direct and the rest is up to you. Other holiday companies such as **www.francenetvillas.com** and **www.somethingspecial.co.uk** are also worthy of consideration. Again, you should consider whether it is not better to come clean about letting income. Teams of tax officers from both sides of the Channel trawl internet sites, and it would be difficult to persuade the tax authorities that your advertisements have generated no response.

Support from regional tourist boards

Regional tourist boards compile and maintain lists of suitable holiday accommodation. Their generally well-produced brochures are available at tourist information centres or through the post. As the principal function of the tourist board is to develop tourism within their area, their charges for including entries in their publications are modest.

The properties and facilities they promote are divided into sections which include small hotels, campsites, chalets and mobile home parks, rural *gîtes*, bed and breakfast accommodation, group accommodation and holiday centres. Whilst in the UK one marketing trend is to promote some accommodation as 'adults only', the French prefer to promote *gîtes* which are particularly suitable for children.

In order to qualify for a tourist board listing, property owners need to comply with the requirements on quality and contract demanded by the board. Accommodation is often graded according to a number of 'keys' (from one to five) depending on the facilities available. One key would denote something fairly basic and five keys deluxe facilities. Tariffs are set accordingly.

The boards are very keen to avoid misunderstandings. Where this applies to the letting contract, they will insist there is a written contract for the let which is signed by both parties. The contract will include the dates and the price agreed, the complete address of the accommodation, the name and address of the proprietor, the letting agent, and the number of persons in the holiday party. The contract must also include a detailed description of the property and its facilities.

The boards can act as arbiters in case of conflicts between the contracted parties. The intention is, of course, to bring any dispute to a prompt and satisfactory conclusion. The boards will only intervene if the letting contract has been signed by both the proprietor and the lessee and if all claims are formulated within 48 hours of the beginning of the holiday. Partly with this in mind, the boards also define a list of permissible supplementary charges, i.e. those charges that can be fairly applied in addition to the published rental price. Whilst, for instance, it is reasonable for the owner to make a supplementary charge for linen and cleaning, he may not do so for gas and electricity. Any cleaning charge (*option aménage*) must be mentioned in the description of the accommodation.

Market auditing

This is not so much a business plan as an assessment of the 'buy to let' market in your chosen area, together with a serious evaluation of what is achievable. You should:

- Check out the opposition. Compare on a 'like-for-like basis' similar properties in similar locations. Find out what the 'opposition' are charging and relate this to the quality they provide. Begin by looking at internet advertising, properties promoted in magazines and newsprint and through estate agents and local small ads. This should provide an overview. When that is in place, begin to study your market on the 'ground'. This means making a collection of promotional material and personally checking out some of the properties available to let.
- Seriously consider becoming a holiday tenant yourself. Surprisingly few people entering the 'buy to let' market do this, which is every bit as sensible as buying a car without a test drive.
- Consider networking with others in the 'buy to let' market. In essence this is attaching yourself to a 'self-help' group and learning from them. It is best to be straightforward about this. You may be surprised just how willing others are to share their knowledge. But beware of claims as to letting income that are at odds with the information you already have.
- Consider building the network into a 'consortium' where mutual self-help and self-interest can be productive in terms of an 'early warning system' for undesirable tenants, and can produce savings in areas such as joint promotional initiatives, and an interchange of bookings. Remember it is always better to pass on business rather than risk customer disappointment. This can also create the impression that your letting business has an exclusivity which, in itself, could help generate further bookings.

- Make an appraisal of your possible client base. This will be partly determined by the locale and the kind of accommodation you provide.
- Carefully consider how much you should charge. It could be a mistake to simply go for the maximum the market can stand or to believe the wealthiest customers will also be the best customers. Equally there may be problems if you decide to deal exclusively in the 'cheap and cheerful'. Trade associations associated with the leisure/holiday rental industry compete fiercely for the 'young family market'. This is because they recognise that here they are most likely to achieve a reasonable and trouble-free return.

Setting business and personal parameters

Most UK people involved in the French 'buy to let' market have some idea that they would like to have some enjoyment of the property themselves. This may be either on a regular basis or part of longer-term retirement plans.

It is important to be both flexible and imaginative. What happens if, for instance, the letting side of the business becomes so successful that you never enjoy the property yourself? Alternatively, if you want to run a low-key business (perhaps only letting the property to family and close friends), are you really going to enjoy the property for that significant number of unbooked weeks there may be in the year? The alternative is to leave the property unoccupied for long periods.

Some of the most successful 'buy to let' businesses have been developed cautiously, perhaps over a number of years, on a 'word of mouth' basis. This requires patience, but the rewards may make it worthwhile. Imagine the benefits of a sustainable list of hand-picked customers who you can genuinely rely on to respect your property. But, in order to achieve this, you may well have to set your charges accordingly.

Medium and long-term strategies should also be considered. Is your first 'buy to let' to be the 'acorn' which founds a business dynasty? Do you regard your investment as primarily in bricks and mortar or as a way of generating additional income? The important thing is to be aware of what your business and personal parameters are, and to refer to them when circumstances seem to distort the balance. A 'buy to let' business is likely to take on a life of its own. Maintaining your business and personal parameters should help you avoid being driven by events.

Business planning

Letting businesses fail for one, or a combination of, the following factors:

- *Under-capitalisation.* It is important to be realistic about the costs. This goes way beyond the acquisition of the property. Try to estimate your costs for the first year. These are likely to include refurbishment and marketing, taxes, utilities, maintenance, wages and insurance. It is better to buy a cheaper property that can be adapted for letting purposes within your budget rather than overreaching yourself. You should also consider the value of your own efforts. If your 'profit' at the year end is €5,000 but you have invested 1,000 hours of your own labour in the business, then you have been working for €5 an hour – below the minimum wage in England and France. Whilst, in the first year, this may not be too much of a disappointment, the danger is that a pattern may have been set.
- *Great expectations.* It is easy to make business assumptions that are not borne out by good evidence. In the 'buy to let' business these can include false assumptions about the letting season and how much, or how little, to charge outside the main holiday period. If you ask too much, the bookings will fail to materialise; too little and your income will be subsumed by running costs.
- *Cash flow.* Cash flow problems are the biggest single reason

why businesses go under. You may pay all your bills on time but that is not the way of the world. Never pay for work that has not been completed.

● *Poor development planning.* Flexibility needs building into your business development planning. Are you prepared, for instance, to turn down enquiries because you do not have the dates available? It is better to send a customer elsewhere, or to offer an alternative date (at a very competitive price) rather than disappoint him. If your letting business is successful, how rapidly will you be able to move to expanding it? Good forward planning includes having backers or partners in place for business development.

Contingency planning

Whilst it is impossible to anticipate all eventualities, those who enter the buying to rent business should be able to predict certain scenarios. What happens, for instance, if your property suffers from burst pipes or a leaky swimming pool? The way you respond to this – in terms of paying refunds and/or putting the problems right – will establish your business reputation. How many holidaymakers' most positive impression comes from something which has gone wrong but which is dealt with promptly and effectively? If you are running the business yourself, a list of local people who can provide the kind of prompt and efficient service that can keep your customers' holiday on track should perhaps be the first item on your 'to do' list (see below).

'To do' lists

Start by working backwards from the date that you hope to begin running your letting business.

Summer holidays are most frequently sold in January and winter breaks in September. Your promotional material must

127

therefore be prepared prior to those deadlines. Ahead of marketing you will require pictures and a full description of the premises. You will also need to have considered model contracts and a pricing strategy.

Your pricing strategy will only work if based on a local market audit. This audit is not only about competing in the buy to rent sector but also about the support resources available locally – such as electricians, plumbers and swimming pool technicians.

Your customers are going to value good information. Your 'to do' lists should therefore include accurate information about route finding, local entertainment, history and culture. Although this mostly means the days and dates of local markets, the distance to the nearest McDonalds and how to tune the satellite TV to *Coronation Street*, it is nevertheless important. And, whilst not necessarily part of your promotional pack, this kind of information should be available, perhaps in a plastic loose-leaf folder at the premises.

SETTING UP YOUR COMPANY

It is important to remember the distinction between an individual and a company. Each has a separate legal identity, different responsibilities, and a different tax burden.

The professional advisers

A *gîte* business is an obvious choice for those wishing to maximise the profitability of their French property assets. Compared with the bureaucratic nightmare of setting up any other kind of business, a *gîte* is also wrapped in rather less red tape.

The penalties, however, for making even honest mistakes can be enormous. For instance, trading before registration formalities are complete can cost you a fine of €16,000. Theoretically, you could also have your equipment confiscated, be deported or imprisoned, and be banned from carrying on any other trading activity in France for three years. In practice, it is rare for any of these sanctions to be applied. Nevertheless, it is important to obtain appropriate legal advice before making any transactions that could be construed as trading.

An early point of contact will be the *notaire*. Even if you intend to work from home you will be required to set up the business formally and to follow registration procedures. The local town halls (*mairies*) can also provide valuable advice.

You should also contact:

The French Chamber of Commerce,
21 Darkmouth Street,
Westminster,
London.
SW1H9HP
Tel : 020 7304 4040

The British Business Centre
BP2114700
Falaise
Tel : 0331 40 05 77

The *notaire*

The *notaire*, again, acts on behalf of all parties to have contract for the purchase of a business or a commercial property. The final stage of contract – the *acte de vente* – can only be legally completed by a *notaire*.

The *agent immobilier*

Most business sales are handled in the early stages by an *agent immobilier*. He draws up preliminary contracts and can complete all formalities except the *acte de vente*.

The *avocat* or *conseil juristique*

The closest equivalent to these professionals in the UK are specialist legal executives. Their offices are most commonly found in the larger cities.

Since 1991 the role of the *avocat* and the *conseil* have been formally identical. Like the *agent immobilier*, he can complete all formalities except for authenticating the final contract.

For the purchase of an existing business there are distinct advantages in using the services of an *avocat*:

- They are invariably specialists at setting up different kinds of companies, and often work exclusively in the commercial area.
- They offer advice on commercial and fiscal matters.
- They will have an up-to-date understanding of civil and employment legislation.
- They charge an agreed rate which is often cheaper than the commission rates charged by an agent *immobilier* or *notaire*.

WHAT KIND OF COMPANY?

French law allows a bewildering range of different kinds of companies. Each has a separate legal identity. The most common are as follows:

Société à Responsabilité Limitée

Very similar to a UK-style limited company. Liability is limited to at least two, and no more than 50 shareholders, who are expected to have an annual general meeting. The minimum legal share capital is €8,000.

Although it may seem rather technical, this is probably the best option for the husband and wife team who intend to work mainly at home. The principal advantage is that liability is limited to the share capital. So, in the event of the company ceasing to trade, the individual shareholders (unless it can be proved that they have been reckless or dishonest) will not face bankruptcy.

Enterprise unipersonnelle à responsabilité limitée

This is another type of limited company for a single shareholder with €8,000 share capital. This form of limited liability is the sensible option for an individual working from home.

Enterprise individuelle

This is similar to the UK sole trader. This is a low-cost option to set up, but liability is unlimited. It is really only suitable for a part-time or low turnover business, but it remains the most common option for those who are choosing to work from home. Common options are, however, not always the most sensible. And owners of *gîte* businesses should earnestly consider whether a French-style limited company would not be both safer and more appropriate.

Société Civile

This style of company requires at least two main shareholders. No shareholding capital is involved, but liability is apportioned according to the number of shares held. This format is most common when a business is based on land ownership. It should be an option seriously considered by those contemplating a 'buy to let' business.

Société en Commandite

This is a hybrid company set up involving both active and sleeping partners. Active partners are fully liable, but for sleeping partners, liability is limited to the amount they have put into the business. This option should be considered by those contemplating 'buy to let' where additional financial support will come from friends and relatives.

Société en nom collectif

Here, there are no minimum capital restrictions for at least two shareholders. These shareholders are responsible for company debts but are treated as sole traders for tax and social security purposes.

Société anonyme

This is a common format for companies who hope to attract venture capital in return for a possible high turnover and large profits. There are at least seven shareholders with a minimum total shareholding of €35,000. Shares may be bought on a subscription basis over a period of five years.

Purchasing property through an off-shore company

The difficulty here is that any off-shore company located in a territory that has not signed the convention with France for combating fiscal fraud will pay an additional levy on the value of the property. Worse still, the company will be charged French income tax at the rate of three times the letting value of the property. Neither the Channel Islands nor the Isle of Man have signed the necessary convention; those which have include the Irish Republic, Mauritius, Singapore, Trinidad and Tobago, and Togo.

An off-shore company located in one of these territories does present a possible financial advantage but this needs to be weighed against the ongoing cost of running an off-shore company. Those considering approaching the French 'buy to let' market in this way should take specialist advice.

Purchasing property through a UK company

This is not normally done because a UK company, whether it makes any profit in France or not, pays corporation tax in France. This tax is due simply because the company holds the property. Another disadvantage is that the French tax authorities can still require you to submit company accounts in France each year. Worse, you will still be liable to pay French taxes.

The principal advantage of purchasing French property through a UK company is that, as long as the shareholders remain domiciled in the UK, French inheritance rules in the favour of children can be avoided.

The audit

With very few exceptions, businesses registered on French soil must present an annual audited statement to the local commercial court. The requirements are:

- *A detailed balance sheet.* This lists fixed assets, current assets, and prepaid expenses. Loss provision, accounts due, allowable expenses and deferred expenses appear on the debit side.
- *A statement of income.* This details expenses and revenues that come from trading and financial transactions.
- *An auditor's statement.* This includes familiar phrases about 'the true and fair view' of the business's financial situation.

All registered companies are required by law to appoint an approved statutory auditor. They have to be independent of the client company and may not be involved in preparing the financial statements on which they report. Auditors are normally appointed for a six-year term. The following organisation can help with detailed inquiries:

The Société Accredite de Representation Français
2 Rue des Petits Pères
75002 Paris

Succersale

This amounts to a branch office. Formalities are limited to registering the company and its articles of incorporation. The French branch office keeps independent accounts. Trading practices, tax, and social security matters become subject to French law.

The definition of what constitutes a *succersale* is complex. Essentially, the French authorities will look at the way the business is conducted. Pointers include:

- Are contracts, invoices and receipts issued locally?
- Is at least one member of the branch staff resident in France for most of the year?
- Does a local manager conduct business negotiations directly with customers?

The advantages of the branch office include:

- The lack of expense and formality required to establish it.
- The branch office's profits and losses can be taken into account in assessing the parent company's income.

Subsidaire

The alternative to a branch office is the *subsidaire* – literally the subsidiary. This is characterised by the branch's subsidiary decision-making and financial control of the parent company. It is nevertheless fully registered as a French company and subject to French law and taxation.

The subsidiary is more complex and expensive to establish than the branch office. However, it has advantages:

- It has greater management flexibility because of its autonomous legal status.
- Parent company liability is limited to a modest stake in the

subsidiary's capital.

- The subsidiary can pay the parent company for financial and technical services. The costs can be deducted from taxable income.
- The subsidiary allows the parent company to co-operate with third parties in France who acquire holdings.

The *subsidaire* is worth considering for those who are likely to expand and develop their 'buy to let' business. It is equally valid if your principal source of income is from a UK-based company – particularly if you are a shareholder of that company.

Bureau de Liaison

This is sometimes called a shop window. It is the legal form that allows foreign businesses to communicate with potential customers – normally through advertising.

The *bureau de liaison* requires the minimum formalities, and is not normally subject to French corporation tax. In order to comply with EU regulations, a French bureau must not undertake any commercial, industrial or service activity. Officially, activities are limited to making contact, surveying the market and advertising.

Any staff employed by a bureau should not have decision-making autonomy or carry out normal management operations. In terms of 'buy to let' the *bureau de liaison* has possibilities. The French authorities will however expect you to demonstrate clearly that the rules which define the bureau are adhered to.

Set-up costs and formalities

The French government has been accused of not making it easy for foreigners to set up business in France. Since 1 January 1992, however, the procedure has been simplified.

In theory at least, the UK businessman should have no more problems than his French counterpart. In practice, however, this is rarely the case. Setting up a 'buy to let' business in France requires not only careful planning and attention to detail but a fair measure of patience. If your ability in the French language is as limited as your patience; you are well advised to appoint a French *avocat* or agent to help unravel the red tape.

Registration

You are required to register your new business at the *Registre du Commerce* within two weeks of starting to trade. To do this you will require:

- A company statute which defines the business in terms of its legal structure, share capital, trading address and activity.
- Proof that share capital has been paid to a *notaire* or deposited in a French bank.
- Documents of incorporation, which are sent to an administrative department – the *Centre de Formalities des Enterprises* – and to the commercial court (*Greffe du Tribunal du Commerce*) which, in turn, informs the tax and social security departments that you are in business.
- A notice of incorporation for publication in a local register – the bulletin of civil and commercial properties.
- Standard form notices for local newspapers.
- An application to register with the *Répertoire des Métiers* (Trade Register), the *Chambre de Commerce et l'Industrie* (Chamber of Commerce and Industry), and possibly with local trade associations.

Theoretically, you could deal with all these matters yourself. It is recommended however that you take professional advice. French bureaucracy is not noted for encouraging individualism. Many of the documents need to be prepared in a precise form and will be returned if they are incomplete or imprecise.

Registration Fees

There are both fixed and flexible charges. According to one trade survey, the average cost of completing business set-up formalities in 2004 was €1,300. A typical breakdown of the costs would be:

Registering a limited company	€ 200
Tax on authorised share capital outlay	€ 65
Incorporation fees for a limited company	€ 500
Legal announcement print costs	€ 170
Professional services	€ 400
Total	€1335

BUYING COMMERCIAL PROPERTY

Fonds de commerce

The legal process for buying business premises is similar to that of the purchase of domestic property. However, there is a significant difference. In French law the property is a separate entity to the business itself. The business – the *fonds de commerce* – includes the trading name, licences, vehicles, fixtures and fittings, stock and intangible assets, and goodwill.

The purchase of the *fonds de commerce* is, in effect, a separate contract. The business can sometimes be sold, or reassigned, without the property itself changing hands.

The preliminary contract

The contract for the purchase of commercial property includes the following elements:

- agreed price and method of payment
- a deposit – normally 10% of the agreed price – which is held by the seller's agent or a *notaire*

- the legal identification of the property itself and the vendors and purchasers
- a description of any additional rights or restrictions that apply to the property
- the vendor's declaration that the property is sold with vacant possession
- an agreed date of completion
- any special conditions (*clauses suspensives*) that will terminate the transaction: one such may be that the deal is subject to the buyer raising a loan or mortgage. As with domestic property, this protects the deposit if the deal cannot be financed.

FINANCING THE BUSINESS

The formal business plan

French banks should be approached with a business plan. This should be prepared to professional standards and drafted in French.

This plan will include:

- a market evaluation
- a full description of the intended trading operation
- details of intended capital purchases, including property leases
- the intended legal format and constitution of the company
- cash flow forecasts
- a full asset and investment profile
- a forecast of accounts for the first three years of trading. For this you do not so much require a crystal ball as the application of a formula which begins with something perhaps slightly better than breaking even and concludes with a note of incautious optimism.

For anything more than the most modest business venture, this information should be completed by an accountant (*un comptable*) or a professional auditor (*un commissaire aux comptes*).

Business loans

Business loans should be approached rather differently from those applicable to a normal loan or mortgage for the purposes of buying a property. The distinction is that in this instance, although a property may be required security, it is the business (which may have limited liability) that requires the finance.

A UK bank

A UK bank will approach the matter in much the same way as they would for setting up a UK business, but are likely to require additional security and safeguards.

The venture capital sector

One way in which French companies raise money is through the circulation of a promotional prospectus on the capital markets. This accounts for around 40% of credit and short-term finance. Rates of interest are competitive.

A French bank

French banks offer a number of arrangements. The principal forms of finance generally amount to loans or leasing contracts for between two and 20 years. Loans are available for up to 80% of the total investment, subject to depreciation, stock and equipment.

When the business involves a property purchase, even where this is domestic premises used as a small business place, the loan will invariably be secured against the property.

Sometimes, 100% finance is available for certain leasing

arrangements. In this case, a leasing company owns the premises for the duration of the lease, but the tenant has the right to buy when the lease contract is terminated. French banks will normally require the following guarantees:

- a charge on the business
- a mortgage on the property
- a charge on certain items of equipment
- an inventory of possessions
- insurance cover assigned to the bank.

Cheaper loans

Loans for smaller amounts, which must not add up to more than 50% of the business, can sometimes be obtained at preferential rates from trade organisations.

Another form of loan is possible if you join a franchise network. In this case, a bank will accept guarantees from a mutual guarantee society set up on behalf of the franchise operators. In some cases, it is possible to obtain a loan that includes the cost of joining the network.

Tax breaks and incentives

The French government is keen to encourage employment and to support investments in the country. This means:

- Government-subsidised loans are available to some craftsmen and traders.
- Industrial business grants and subsidies are available on a regional basis. This is similar to the regional aid programme operating in the UK. It is EU funded and intended to help commercial and industrial regeneration. Information is available from the *conseil régionale* in each area.
- Indirect grant aid is available in the form of tax abatement for new businesses. For the first two years 100% abatement on profit taxation applies. This is followed by a sliding scale

that reduces to a 25% abatement in the fifth year.
Independent professionals, and those selling financial
services and insurances, do not enjoy this abatement.

- *Taxes professionnelles* are not levied in the first year. These are
  similar to UK business rates. The bill can vary considerably
  according to location, and exemptions beyond the first year are
  also determined on a local basis.
- Up to 25% of the initial investment in a business can be offset
  against personal income tax. The ceiling here is €1,500 for a
  single person and €3,000 for a married couple.

EMPLOYING OTHERS

Permits

Traditionally all those who sought work in France had to apply
for a work permit (*carte de travail*) and a residence permit
(*carte de sejour*). Applications were sometimes turned down
without reason or right of appeal. This now only applies to non-
EU workers.

Members of the EU are now automatically entitled to renewable
five-year permits, but these still require full documentation.

Working hours

These have been defined since 1982 as:

- A 39 hour working week. Overtime is not mandatory and
  must be paid at enhanced rates. The 'week' has since been
  reduced by two hours but there is now economic pressure to
  reintroduce the 39 hour benchmark.
- Employees cannot be required to work on Sundays.
- The minimum paid holiday allowance is five weeks plus the 11
  national holidays.
- Part-time contracts are notionally pro-rated. In practice, this is
  difficult to administer and enforce. Most French people

take their holidays in August and most businesses close on bank holidays. For all practical purposes, much commercial activity grinds to a halt for seven weeks each year.

Wages

France has minimum wage legislation. However, this has been largely unenforceable since France began to suffer significant unemployment problems a few years ago.

Theoretically the legal minimum wage is linked to the cost of living index:

- Until recently the legal minimum was €5.77 an hour.
- Semi-skilled workers normally receive a minimum wage 15 to 20% higher than the legal minimum. Skilled workers receive 40 to 50% more.
- Management salaries are generally within the range of €3,500 to €8,500 per month.
- Special conditions apply to those working in the hotel and catering sectors.

Wages tax (*taxes sur les salaires*)

This is regarded as a clawback tax – rather similar to Class Four National Insurance contributions in the UK. Nobody knows quite why it exists other than that it is assumed that everybody is 'fiddling' a little. It is applied only to businesses not required to register for *TVA*. Recently the following rates were applied:

Table 8.1 Wages tax

Company wage bill	Percentage charge
0 to €5,700	4.25
€5,701 to €11,075	8.50
€11,076 and above	9.50

Contracts of employment

Everyone employed in France is entitled to a written contract. This covers three main areas:

- the job description
- the agreed wage
- the legal position of the employee in terms of responsibilities within the company.

The contract can be for a fixed or an indefinite period. Any contract that does not state the fixed period of employment is deemed to be indefinite.

Stringent warnings and procedures have to be followed before an employee can be dismissed from an indefinite contract. This is intended to prevent arbitrary dismissals. The only genuine reasons accepted are proven criminality, misconduct or professional inadequacy. Disputed cases are judged by tribunal. Wrongful dismissal invariably brings a substantial entitlement to compensation.

Fixed contracts should be for no longer than two years. Unless the employer can prove just cause for an earlier termination, the employee will receive a compensation sum at least equal to the remaining portion of his contract.

Welfare payments

Foreign companies with a French base have to contribute to employment, health and retirement schemes on behalf of their employees. Those in employment also make their own contributions. The only exception to this is in the case of a temporary employment from other EC countries.

Contributions by and on behalf of part-time workers are pro-rated according to the hours worked. In practice, this is usually worked out as a proportion of income during a 'standard' month.

Both employer's and employee's contributions to the French

welfare system have been traditionally higher than in the UK. Recently, for example:

- The employer's contribution to sickness, maternity and disability benefit was 12.6%, with the employee contributing 5.9%.

- The employer's contribution to state pensions contributions was set at 8.2%, with the employee contributing 7.6%.

Communications

Although the French communication systems are as technically advanced as those in the UK, the failure rate is rather higher. This is at least partly because of the regular interruptions to the electricity supply. There is also the problem that demand has constantly exceeded the number of lines, channels and bandwidth available. And, those used to dialling UK 0845 numbers as access to email services will find they are not be able to do so in France. The best solution is probably to sign up with a French company such as **www.wanadoo.fr**

SETTING UP THE BUSINESS IN THE HOME

Domestic and commercial property

The situation is similar to that found in the UK. Often only a fine line distinguishes domestic from commercial premises, but the judgements as to which is which are usually based on the property itself and where it is situated.

A general rule is that each building is liable for rates, either as domestic or commercial premises. The fact that your home may also be your registered office does not mean that the premises themselves are commercial. That is determined by the scale and type of activity carried on there.

In certain circumstances, part of the domestic property could become liable for *taxes professionnelles* – business rates. This would apply typically, perhaps, to a doctor or architect, when part of his domestic premises were set aside and equipped exclusively for business use.

Another complexity arises from the fact that if you have a business in France you must also have a registered office. This is not necessarily either your home or your business premises. For the first two years, for instance, you can register your business at the office of your *notaire*.

Business and domestic loans

This is normally straightforward. For those buying to rent, you would probably have a normal domestic mortgage for which the security is the property itself. Consider the position, however, of taking over an existing *gîte* business, a *colonie de vacances* or a hotel. Here the value of the business may be as great as, or greater, than the property itself.

You also have the theoretical options of letting part or all of the property and maintaining part or all of the business. There is also the possibility of keeping the property for yourself but selling all or part of the business element. According to circumstances, therefore, you may be eligible for a business loan, which in itself could be a deciding factor in the tax breaks and other incentives for which you are eligible.

But planning a business, in itself, is not sufficient to convince a lender that you should be eligible for a business loan. A self-employed writer, artist or craftsman, working from home, would normally be expected to apply for a domestic mortgage. This would probably still be true even if part of the premises were to be let for part of the year. Your eligibility for lower rate loans, tax breaks and other incentives, will ultimately depend not only on exactly what you propose to do but on the way you approach it.

Property development

This has been described as a grey area. Adding an extra room, for instance, would probably not affect the tax, rates, or loan situation. The assumption would be that the property was still primarily residential. Plans to build a studio that is wholly separate from the house could be interpreted differently.

Again the local *mairie* and chamber of commerce can advise. And once your business is registered with them, it is usually possible to get a quick ruling.

Other checks and safeguards

If you are living at the property and letting part of it to holiday customers you will be deemed by the French authorities to be 'working from home'.

You should therefore make sure that:

- You have obtained your residence card from the local *préfecture de police.*
- You have informed your *notaire* at the time of the property purchase that you intend to use all/part of the premises for business purposes. This will ensure that the terms of your freehold lease do not exclude business activities. This is rarely a problem – unless the property is held under one of the many French formats of multi- or co-ownership.
- You have checked that your type of business can legally be run from home.
- In the larger cities, by-laws forbid particular forms of businesses on domestic premises. Generally, the French tradition of personal liberty is upheld, but you would be unwise to think these have extended to noisy night-shifts in a workshop in the middle of a housing estate.
- Your insurance cover is extended to appropriate business usage, and in certain cases, public liability.

9

Marketing and Managing Your Business

There have been many books written on how to market a
business. In terms of buying to let – particularly if you are
entering the holiday letting business – the following
considerations may be considered as paramount:

- establishing your company profile and presenting it effectively
- reaching the customer through advertising and publicity
- maintaining a competitive edge
- developing and utilising a customer database
- encouraging customer feedback and taking note of it.

THE COMPANY PROFILE AND PRESENTATION

Even the most modest 'buy to let' business should be presented
professionally. Every letterhead, photograph, poster, flyer,
website, and document you use represents your company. It is
worth taking time and care to get this right. The general rules are:

- keep things simple
- keep the same logos, fonts and formats in all your
  documentation
- update your materials annually
- make sure all enquiries are dealt with promptly
- see criticism as an opportunity rather than an attack
- remember everyone who represents you (for instance when the
  telephone is answered) also represents the business. First
  impressions are crucial
- always keep your promises.

ADVERTISING AND PUBLICITY

You will have already considered advertising as part of your business plan. The most effective advertising, however, need not be expensive. Always remember:

- Free publicity – newspapers and magazines are always on the lookout for ideas to fill their pages.
- Is there something unusual about the property that you have bought?
- Is there something distinctive about the area in which the property is sited?
- What do you know about local history, traditions, and events?

Advertising should always begin at home. This can mean a card in your local newsagent's window informing friends and family that the property is available and making use of noticeboards in supermarkets and staffrooms.

An internet site is now an essential tool for effective promotion. You could begin by buying your own domain (these are available from around €25 for two years). If your own computer skills are limited, you do not necessarily need the expertise of a professional website designer. Students, even school children, are often more than capable of building a basic but effective site. Again, keep it simple. Make sure your first page loads quickly and that all the basic information is readily accessible. Limit the number of pictures you use (they can take ages to load) and make sure you include an email address and a standard form of contract. Resist flashing lights and animation. Remember keywords and hyperlinks, and make sure you register with the popular search engines.

For newspaper advertising try your local (UK) paper first. For some inexplicable reason, people are always more likely to trust people from their own neighbourhood. In terms of national advertising in the UK, the rates can be expensive. Sunday newspapers – particularly the *The Sunday Telegraph, Mail* on Sunday and *The Sunday Times* – do, however, deliver the goods. *The Daily Telegraph* is also hugely effective in this market place. Never advertise before you are ready to take bookings. This is not only wasteful but is likely to alienate customers. Take note of where customer responses come from so you can perform your own audit of 'best value' in advertising. Before you place any advertising be very sure of what you want to say. Consider what your selling points are and how to put them across most effectively. Remember also that the way you phrase your advertisement and where you place it will determine the nature of customer response. If you are targeting a particular market area it is best to think this through very carefully.

Agency and Umbrella Marketing

There are a number of agencies and holiday organisations who, for a suitable fee, will provide everything from simple promotion on a website and/or in a brochure, to a full service. Their fees vary considerably – up to 25% of the advertised holiday price in some cases – and, therefore, they may not provide the best way forward for everyone. A list of some of the longest established companies is included in the final chapter.

The Competitive Edge

Although most people have a fairly clear idea of the value of their UK property, it is surprising how many will buy in France without having studied the property market place. When this is translated into 'buy to let' the problem is multiplied.

Part of the problem is because French estate agents are likely to give a distorted impression of just how easy buying to let is. But the market is becoming ever more competitive. Holiday clients do not want a 'home from home' any more: they want more than that. Even rural *gîtes* will often feature:

- quality fixtures and fittings, including the full range of kitchen appliances
- off-road parking for two vehicles
- caretaking and cleaning services
- satellite television
- a brick-built barbecue and children's play area
- a swimming pool, particularly if the property is located in the southern half of France.

A *gîte* is generally expected to be comparable with the kind of quality expected in a three star hotel, but, at the same time, offer rather more independence to the holidaymakers. Rather less, of course, is expected in the larger cities, where the accommodation and facilities will inevitably be more limited. However, the expectation is still that the property will be well finished, furnished and maintained.

To be competitive, you will not only have to provide what the market demands but pitch your scale of charges realistically.

THE CUSTOMER DATABASE

The value of a customer database is, perhaps, not fully appreciated unless you are buying into an existing 'buy to let' business. A part of the 'goodwill' of the sale should be the customer database, and if this is to be exclusive to the new owner it could add up to 10% to the sale price.

The French do not undervalue databases: even some campsites will send out seasonal booking information to previous customers. All good computer-based software – such as Access (part of the Microsoft Office Suite) will allow you to divide your entries into appropriate fields which can be separately referenced later. Every enquiry should be logged for future promotional purposes. When enquiries become bookings you should set up entry fields which include:

- name of customer

- name of customer's partner
- names and ages of children
- address and nationality
- telephone number and email address
- record of payments
- record of previous bookings with you
- source of advertising which prompted the enquiry.

The database will take the guesswork out of profiling your customers. It will tell you not only who they are but how they found out about you. This, in turn, will help you identify the most effective form of advertising. There may also be some surprises. One *gîte* owner in Toulon was surprised to find that almost 30% of his customers were Dutch couples with children at the lower end of the teenage range. There was no reasonable demographic or promotional reason for this. Further investigation revealed that all the children attended the same élite residential music school and that their parents came together as a group once a year for a series of concerts.

A similar anomaly was resolved by the owner of a camping park in Southern Brittany. The park had six log cabin style holiday cottages which generated some welcome autumn business from middle-aged Spaniards. Again, there was no common demography and so the park owner began asking questions, as unobtrusively as possible, about the occupations and so on of those who were booking his accommodation. Again, there was no obvious thread to follow. The mystery was however solved by a small booklet left behind by one of his Spanish visitors. His visitors were clearly all members of a religious fellowship who made an annual autumn tour of three of Europe's most sacred sites (Santiago de Compostella, Lourdes, and Mont Saint Michel). The route through Southern Brittany was totally arbitrary, but pleasantly scenic, and just happened to provide enough accommodation for the whole party.

FEEDBACK AND DEVELOPMENT

Feedback from customers is a crucial measure of the success of the business and, when taken with database information, can provide pointers for future development.

Feedback should be both formal and informal. During a holiday stay, somebody should be available to monitor the comments and complaints of the visitors. A standard form should also be provided for their written observations. To make this most valuable the form should be divided into sections which deal with:

- comments on the property itself
- comments on the locale
- comments on the services provided
- suggestions for modifications and/or improvements
- perceptions as to value for money.

In addition to providing valuable insights to the property owner the provision of a feedback form creates the impression of being prepared to work with guests to improve standards year on year.

LOCAL TIE-INS

The owners of 'buy to let' property should consider the benefits to themselves and their customers of arranging various local tie-ins. This could include negotiated discounts with local restaurants and those providing leisure facilities.

This really is a case of 'everyone wins'. Some UK owners in France have been particularly creative. Free tours of local wine 'caves' have been supplemented with a special delivery service on the last day of the holiday booking. Another scheme has unused portions of ski lift tickets transferable to a local pizza restaurant. But perhaps the most imaginative of all is one scheme which allows credits to be gained by shopping at certain local establishments which can later be traded for tickets to watch the local football team, go ice-skating or swimming (according to season), or for a hamper of local delicacies that will be delivered to a UK address at Christmas.

MANAGING THE BUSINESS

It is sometimes said there are only two styles of management:

- that learned in the private sector with emphasis on getting it right
- that learned in the public sector with emphasis on not getting it wrong.

The corollary to this is that former public sector managers should never try their hand at business.

These may be clichés, but there can be little doubt that a personal management style evolves through experience. But, whatever that experience is, it should clearly reflect what you are trying to achieve.

In the buy to let sector you need to be able to respond quickly to changing market conditions. This is only possible if those you employ are prepared to make these changes with you. It is also about the management of time. Time is both money and efficiency. Try to learn from your mistakes and constantly ask yourself if you are doing things in the best possible way.

Perhaps the best, and most enduring, example of poor management is the Basil Fawlty model of unvarying overreaction. Sadly, there are worthy examples of this style of management in the buy to let industry :

- One *gîte* owner in Provence famously responds to every complaint with a tirade of personal abuse. Another owner, in Normandy, delights in informing his visitors just how stupid most of his 'other customers' are.
- A *gîte* owner in the Dordogne approached the holiday family on the last day of their stay and returned just

€75 of their €200 breakages deposit. Obviously there was an inquest about this with the *gîte* owner claiming that the €125 would cover the cost of electricity, the few logs they had used in the fireplace and the packet of toilet rolls that he had provided. And, whilst the holidaymakers stood open mouthed in disbelief, he produced a sachet of cleaning fluid for the floors and told them that it would be helpful if they vacated the premises two hours earlier than had previously been agreed as his next guests were coming early. This is a classic example of poor business practice. It absolutely guaranteed that not only would these customers never return but that they would tell all their friends, and a certain writer of books about French property, about their experience.

10

The Internet

The internet is possibly the quickest way of obtaining information in any given area. From your home, you can book and pay for your holidays, or check on the climate and current weather for almost everywhere in the world.

BUYING A PROPERTY

There are many internet sites devoted to selling property in France. The following were amongst the best known:

http://www.green-acre.com

This company not only lists available property, but if you register with them (free of charge) it will search for a property in the area/price range you designate. It has versions in both French and English and can act as an estate agent for you if you wish to sell your property.

http://www.french-property.com

A number of French estate agents use this site to advertise those properties they think will be attractive to UK buyers. This site has possibly the most properties for sale and at prices to suit all pockets. It will also put you in touch with other people looking for property so you can exchange ideas etc. and you can buy books like this one through their bookshop.

http://www.french-property-news.com

A visit to this single site would permit you to find the property you wish to buy, be escorted to visit it, have an agent during the purchase process, find a connection to a mortgage broker, get a company to renovate it, another to act as agents for your *gîte*, obtain the services of a gardener and then sell it for you if get tired of it. They offer advice on their 'Legal Tips' page and will send you a regular newsletter.

http://www.frenchproperty.co.uk
Rather upmarket properties for sale, including small estates, and holiday rentals, too.

http://coast-country.com
'The English Estate Agents on the French Riviera' have properties for sale and rent and links to sites offering weather forecasts and Riviera news.

http://www.timeshare-traders.com
Timeshare specialists.

http://www.abimmo.com
A French language site. You need to know the department number of your desired area to begin the search. The site is well signposted and easy to navigate after that.

http://www.123voyage.com
A site with links to many different aspects searching for a property in the right place.

http://www.abelcom.net
Lots of background information on France and your chosen region. Offers properties on a 'number of principal rooms' basis.

RENTING A PROPERTY

You may already be familiar with sites where individual owners advertise their property for short-term rental. These sites featured most frequently in internet searches are:

http://www.cheznous.com
A comprehensive service offering properties from individuals together with travel arrangements, holiday insurance and booking hotels en route to your destination.

http://www.gites-in-france.co.uk
Concerned mainly with *gîtes* for rental or sale.

http://www.webconnection.co.uk
Holiday rental, but with the addition of offering long winter lets – ideal for those who wish to check out their location before buying.

http://www.frenchconnections.co.uk
Self-catering *gîtes* and B&B.

http://www.ghestates.co.uk
Offers 'luxury and secluded holiday accommodation in Charente and Dordogne'.

http://www.chez-oz.com.au
Don't be put off by the title! It's run by an Australian company and has a wide range of *gîtes* on offer.

http://www.propertyinfrance.com
Opening page shows a number of properties for rent in each region. There are properties in all market sectors.

FINANCING THE DEAL

French and UK banks have already been mentioned. The following website can give you an immediate response, at least in principle :

http://www.french-mortgage-connection.co.uk

MANAGING YOUR MONEY

Many UK banks have accounts which can be managed via the internet, but beware the bank that wants to charge you for the software to do it. There are also specialist internet banks.

Cahoot.com is an offshoot of HBSC and offers simple current accounts. **http://www.egg.com** is an offshoot of the Prudential which offers reasonably high interest rates on savings. **http://www.virginone.com** is part of the Royal Bank of Scotland and offers special mortgage/current accounts for those whose salary is paid directly into the account.

Paying bills

Income tax
The Inland Revenue permits you to fill in your tax return online and send it to them electronically. Their web site is:

http://www.inlandrevenue.gov.uk

This site has not always received the best press, especially with those filling in their returns at the last minute.

Standard UK bills

Girobank have a special site for paying bills on UK utilities :

http://www.billspayment.co.uk

RADIO

All the BBC radio broadcasts can be received via **http://www.bbc.co.uk** and via Sky subscription on channels ascending from 851 (Radio 1).

Appendix 1

FURTHER READING

Books

Bed and Breakfast of Character and Charm in France, Fodor's Rivages.

Buying and Renovating Property in France, J. Kater Pollock, Flowerpoll.

Gîtes de France Official Handbook, Gîtes de France.

Buying and Restoring Old Property in France, David Everett, Robert Hale.

Buying and Selling Residential Property in France, Chamber of Commerce.

Can We Afford the Bidet? Elizabeth Morgan, Lennard.

French Dirt, Richard Goodman Pavilion Books.

French or Foe, Polly Platt, Culture Crossings.

French Law for Property Buyers, Kerry Schrader, French Property News.

Home and Dry in France, George East, La Puce Publications.

The Legal Beagle Goes to France, Bill Thomas, Quiller Press.

Live and Work in France, Nicole Prevost Logan, How To Books.

Living as a British Expatriate in France, Chamber of Commerce.

Maison Therapy, Alistair Simpson, New Horizon.

Setting Up a Small Business in France, Chamber of Commerce.

Some of My Best Friends are French, Colin Corder, Shelf Publishing.

Traditional Villages of Rural France, Bill Laws, BCA.

Understanding France, John P. Harris, Papermac.

ENGLISH LANGUAGE NEWSPAPERS AND MAGAZINES

Blue Coast, 32 rue Marechal Joffre, 06000, Nice

Boulevard, Madiatime France SA, 68 Rue des Archives,75003 Paris

France Magazine, Dormer House, Stow-on-the-Wold, Glos. GL54 1BN

French Property News, 2A Lampton Road, London SW20 0LR

Focus on France, Outbound Publishing, I Commercial Rd., Eastbourne BN21 3XQ

Living France, 79 High St., Olney MK46 4EF

The Riviera Reporter, 56 Chemin de Provence, 06250 Mougins

Appendix 2

THE DEPARTMENTS

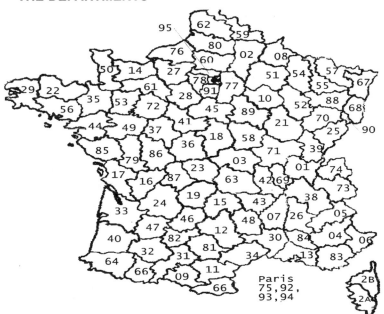

Department No.	Department Name	Area
01	Ain	Rhone-Alps
02	Aisne	North
03	Allier	Auvergne
04	Alpes-de-Haute-Provence	Provence
05	Hautes-Alpes	Provence

06	Alpes-Maritimes	Provence
07	Ardèche	Rhone-Alps
08	Ardennes	North
09	Ariège	Midi-Pyrenees
10	Aube	North
11	Aude	Languedoc
12	Aveyron	Midi-Pyrenees
13	Bouches-du-Rhône	Provence
14	Calvados	Normandy
15	Cantal	Auvergne
16	Charente	Aquitaine
17	Charente Maritime	Aquitaine
18	Cher	Loire
19	Corrèze	Auvergne
21	Côte-d'Or	Burgundy
22	Côtes-d'Armour	Brittany
23	Creuse	Auvergne
24	Dordogne	Aquitaine
25	Doubs	Burgundy
26	Drôme	Rhone-Alps
27	Eure	Normandy
28	Eure-et-Loire	Loire
29	Finistère	Brittany
30	Gard	Languedoc
31	Haute-Garonne	Midi-Pyrenees
32	Gers	Midi-Pyrenees
33	Gironde	Aquitaine
34	Hérault	Languedoc
35	Ille-et-Villaine	Brittany
36	Indre	Loire
37	Indre-et-Loire	Loire
38	Isère	Rhone-Alps
39	Jura	Burgundy
40	Landes	Aquitaine
41	Loir-et-Cher	Loire
42	Loire	Rhone-Alps

44	Loire-Atlantique	Brittany
45	Loiret	Loire
46	Lot-et-Garonne	Midi-Pyrenees
47	Lot-et-Garonne	Aquitaine
48	Lozère	Languedoc
49	Maine-et-Loire	Loire
50	Manche	Normandy
51	Marne	North
52	Haute-Marne	North
53	Haute-Loire	Auvergne
53	Mayenne	Loire
54	Meurthe-et-Moselle	Alsace
55	Meuse	Alsacc
56	Morbihan	Brittany
57	Moselle	Alsace
58	Nièvre	Burgundy
59	Nord	North
60	Oise	North
61	Orne	Normandy
62	Pas-de-Calais	North
63	Puy-de-Dôme	Auvergne
64	Pyrénées-Atlantiques	Aquitaine
65	Haute-Pyrénées	Midi-Pyrenees
66	Pyrénées-Orientales	Languedoc
67	Bas-Rhin	Alsace
68	Haut-Rhin	Alsace
69	Rhône	Rhone-Alps
70	Haute-Saône	Burgundy
71	Saône-et-Loire	Burgundy
72	Sarthe	Loire
73	Savoie	Rhone-Alps
74	Haute-Savoie	Rhone-Alps
75	Paris	Paris
76	Seine-Maritime	Normandy
77	Seine-et-Marne	Paris
78	Yvelines	Paris

79	Deux-Sèvres	Aquitaine
80	Somme	North
81	Tarn	Midi-Pyrenees
82	Tarn-et-Garonne	Midi-Pyrenees
83	Var	Provence
84	Vaucluse	Provence
85	Vendée	Loire
87	Haute-Vienne	Auvergne
88	Vosges	Alsace
89	Yonne	Burgundy
90	Territoire de Belfort	Burgundy
91	Essonne	Paris
92	Hauts-de-Seine	Paris
93	Seine Saint-Denis	Paris
94	Val-de-Marne	Paris
95	Val-d'oise	Paris
96	Vienne	Aquitaine
2A	Corse-du-Sud	Corsica
2B	Haute-Corse	Corsica

Appendix 3

LONG-TERM LETTING CONTRACT

CONTRACT DE LOCATION
Loi No. 89–462 du 6 juillet 1989
LOCAUX VACANTS NON MEUBLES

BAILLEUR (property owner)...
MANDATAIRE (agent/valuer)...
Et LOCATAIRES (tenants)..

Le bailleur loue les locaux et equipements ci-après designes au locataire qui les accepte aux conditions suivantes. *(The owner rents the premises & equipment designated hereafter to the tenant who accepts them subject to the following conditions.)*

LOCAUX (premises)..

... Habitation principale   ... Appartement
... Professionel et Habitational principale... Maison individuelle

DESIGNATION DES LOCAUX ET EQUIPMENTS
PRIVATIFS
....
Garage No. ....   Place de station No. ....
Cave No.   ....   Autre   ....

ENUMERATION DES PARTIES ET EQUIPEMENTS COMMUNES

... Gardiennage   ... Vide-ordures
... Interphone   ... Ascenseur
... Antenne TV collective   ... Chauffage collectif
... Eau chaude collective   ... Espace(s) vert(s)

FIXATION DU LOYER

(There follows a series of legal definitions of the property and its state of repair according to articles 17, 17B and 18 of the law. If in any doubt, consult your solicitor)

DUREE INITIALE DU CONTRAT
(*Initial period of contract*) ....

RAISONS PROFESSIONNELLES OU FAMILIALES DU BAILLEUR
(*Professional or family reasons for contract being less than three years*)
....
....

DATE DE PRISE D'EFFET (*Date contract comes into effect*)
....

MONTANTS DES PAIEMENTS (*Total amount of payments*)

Loyer mensuel (*Monthly rent*)   ....
Taxes (*Taxes*)   ....

Provisions sur charges
(*Provision for charges*)   ....

Total Mensuel (*Monthly total*)   ....

TERMES DE PAIEMENT (*Payment terms*)

Cette somme sera payable d'advance et en totalite le ... de chaque mois.
(*This sum will be payable in full and in advance on the ... of each month.*)

REVISION DE LOYER (*Rent review*)

Le loyer sera revisée chaque année le ...
(*The rent review takes place each year in ...*)

DEPOT DE GARANTIE (Deposit......................

CLAUSE PARTICULIERE (*Special clause*)

....

....

....

HONORAIRES A PARTAGER PAR MOITIE
(*Fees to be equally divided*)

HONORAIRES DE TRANSACTION (*Transaction fees*) ....
HONORAIRES DE REDACTION (*Drafting fees*) ....
FRAIS D'ETAT DES LIEUX (*Local fees*) ....

DOCUMENTS ANNEXES (*Appendices*)
(These could include lists of locally defined charges, extracts from the regulations governing co-ownership local regulations for the recovery of keys and references to neighbourhood rents.)

CLES REMISES (*Keys*)

Nombres de cles remises au locataire ....
(*Number of keys given to tenant*) ....

SIGNATURE DES PARTIES

Fait et signé à .... le .... en ....
originaux dont un remis à chacun des parties qui le reconnait.

.... LE BAILLEUR

.... LE(S) LOCATAIRE(S)
....

.... LA CAUTION

CONDITIONS GENERALES

A. CONTRAT D'UNE DUREE MINIMALE DE 3 OU 6 ANS
(*Contract for a minimum of three or six years*)

* RESILIATION – CONGE (*Termination of lease*)

(The TENANT must give a minimum of three months' notice, in writing. This can be reduced to one month in the case of loss of employment or poor health of a tenant over 60.)
(The OWNER must give a minimum of six months' notice, in writing. This can be reduced in the event that the tenant is not carrying out his obligations.)

* RENOUVELLEMENT (*Renewal*)

(Six months before the end of the contract, the owner can propose renewal of contract in writing. Either : a) for less time, but a minimum of one year, under same conditions as previously. b) For a minimum of three or six further years under conditions to be agreed.)

B. CONTRAT D'UNE DUREE INFERIEURE DE 3 ANS
(*Contract for less than three years*)

(This contract is for a period of not less than one year and only comes into operation if the owner can prove family or professional reasons why it should be so. These reasons must be given on the contract.)

CLAUSE PARTICULIERE CONCERNANT LES LOCAUX CONSTRUITS AVANT DE 1.9.1948
(*clause only for properties constructed before 1.9.48*)

(This deals with the state of repair of the property and the minimum standards it must reach.)

CHARGES (*charges*)

(This clause permits the owner to recover from the tenant such charges as repairs to communal equipment, or taxes which correspond to services from which the tenant benefits. They are to be fixed annually. The owner must provide the tenant with a complete breakdown of the charges at least one month before they are due.)

DEPOT DE GARANTIE (*deposit*)

(The deposit may not exceed 2 months' rent and it must be returned to the tenant not more than 2 months after the keys have been returned. As in English law, it can be used to pay any debts left behind by the tenant etc.)

TRAVAUX EVENTUELS ENTRAINANT MODIFICATION DE LOYER
(*work which could lead to the modification of the rent.*)

a) Work done by the tenant to ensure that the property remains up to minimum standards.

b) Improvements made by the owner.

OBLIGATIONS DU BAILLEUR (*Owner's responsibilities*)

(This includes such things as keeping the property in a good state of repair and keeping receipts for payments and charges.)

OBLIGATIONS DU LOCATAIRE (*Tenant's responsibilities*)

(Including such things as making due payments, keeping the property in good order and permitting access by the owner or his appointed agent at an agreed time.)

CLAUSE RESOLUTOIRE ET CLAUSE PENAL
(*penalty & termination clauses*)

(The main termination clause permits the owner to terminate the contract after two months' non-payment of rent. The main penalty clause permits the owner to recover the cost of an expulsion order against the tenant.)

SOLIDARITE INDIVISIBILITE – ELECTION DE DOMICILE

(The contract is legally binding upon the heirs of either or both parties.)

FRAIS – HONORAIRES (*fees*)

(All fees are joint responsibility.)

Index